The Essence of
Competitive Strategy

The Essence of Management Series

Published titles

The Essence of Total Quality Management
The Essence of Strategic Management
The Essence of International Money
The Essence of Management Accounting
The Essence of Financial Accounting
The Essence of Marketing Research
The Essence of Information Systems
The Essence of Personal Microcomputing
The Essence of Successful Staff Selection
The Essence of Effective Communication
The Essence of Statistics for Business
The Essence of Business Taxation
The Essence of the Economy
The Essence of Mathematics for Business
The Essence of Organizational Behaviour
The Essence of Small Business
The Essence of Business Economics
The Essence of Operations Management
The Essence of Services Marketing
The Essence of International Business
The Essence of Marketing
The Essence of Managing People
The Essence of Change
The Essence of International Marketing
The Essence of Personnel Management and Industrial Relations

Forthcoming titles

The Essence of Public Relations
The Essence of Financial Management
The Essence of Business Law
The Essence of Women in Management
The Essence of Mergers and Acquisitions
The Essence of Influencing Skills
The Essence of Services Management
The Essence of Industrial Marketing
The Essence of Venture Capital and New Ventures

The Essence of Competitive Strategy

WITHDRAWN

David Faulkner 2 9 APR 2023

and

Cliff Bowman

Prentice Hall

New York   London   Toronto   Sydney   Tokyo   Singapore

01442 881900

First published 1995 by
Prentice Hall International (UK) Limited
Campus 400, Maylands Avenue
Hemel Hempstead
Hertfordshire, HP2 7EZ
A division of
Simon & Schuster International Group

Typeset in 10/12pt Palatino by
Keyset Composition, Colchester

Printed and bound in Great Britain by
Hartnolls Limited, Bodmin, Cornwall

Library of Congress Cataloging-in-Publication Data

Faulkner, David, 1938–
    The essence of competitive strategy / David Faulkner and
Cliff Bowman.
        p.   cm. — (The Essence of management series)
    Includes bibliographical references (p.   ) and index.
    ISBN 0-13-291477-8
    1. Competition. 2. Corporate planning. I. Bowman, Cliff.
II. Title. III. Series
HD41.F38   1995
658.4'012 — dc20   94-29722
                                                              CIP

British Library Cataloguing in Publication Data

A catalogue record for this book is available from
the British Library

ISBN 0-13-291477-8 (pbk)

  2 3 4 5   99 98 97 96 95

Contents

1

Introduction

A useful distinction can be made between the content of strategy and the process of strategy. By strategy **content** we mean what the strategy is about: for example, is it corporate-level strategy, or a business unit strategy, or functional or operational strategy (e.g. a marketing strategy)? The **process** of strategy is concerned with the means by which strategy is developed.

1.1 Levels of strategy

There are three distinct levels of strategy as shown in Figure 1.1.

Corporate strategy is the concern of organizations which are a collection of relatively independent businesses, sometimes called Strategic Business Units (SBUs). Corporate strategy is fundamentally concerned with the logic or rationale of the corporation. Put simply, corporate strategies address the questions 'Which businesses should we be in?' and 'How should we run them?'. There are various arguments put forward to justify the multi-SBU corporation:

- **The portfolio argument:** by grouping together separate businesses they can be more effectively managed, particularly with regard to the management of finance. For example, the cash generated by one maturing business unit can be used to fund the development of another unit which is in a phase of rapid growth.

Content

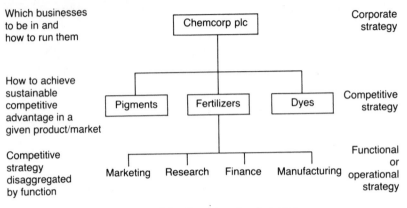

Figure 1.1   The three levels of strategy

- **The synergy argument:** here the rationale for the corporation rests on there being important similarities between SBUs. This permits the sharing of resources between SBUs which helps individual businesses either to lower costs or to compete more effectively in their markets.
- **The core competences argument:** if the corporation has developed a particular capability, this may be 'leveraged' across other business units to gain competitive advantage. For example, Honda's expertise in small four-stroke petrol engines enabled them to move into cars, lawn-mowers and outboard motors.

Competitive strategy is the essential concern of this book, although there are several references in the book to links between competitive and corporate strategy. Competitive strategy, also known as business-level or SBU strategy, is essentially concerned with the competition of products and services in the marketplace. There are three fundamental questions which must be addressed at this level of strategy:

1. Where should we compete? (Which markets, and which segments within those markets should we concentrate on?)
2. What products should we compete with?
3. How will we gain sustainable competitive advantage in these chosen markets?

If the management team does not have answers to these questions, then the business does not have a clear, thought through and understood competitive strategy.

Functional strategy is concerned with interpreting the role of the function or department in delivering the competitive strategy. In this sense, functional strategy is driven by competitive strategy. Thus every competitive strategy can be translated into congruent marketing strategies, financial strategies, personnel strategies and so forth at the functional level.

1.2 The strategy process

The **process** of strategy refers to the way in which the strategy comes about in the organization. Strategies can be deliberately established (through analysis, leading to a plan or a mission for the business) or they can emerge through a series of seemingly unconnected operational-level decisions. In practice few competitive strategies are determined purely by a planned process or a purely emergent process: these are best viewed as two ends of a continuum.

As the rest of the book focuses on the **content** of competitive strategy, in this chapter we will address some of the more significant issues concerning the **process** of strategy.

Unfortunately, it appears that even when a team of managers plans the future direction for the firm, these well-intentioned plans often fail to be realized. The process by which the strategy comes about seems to affect the chances of the strategy being implemented. For example, if the strategy has been drawn up by outside consultants, the members of the executive team may not be particularly committed to implementing the plan (because they were not sufficiently involved in the process). The plan may have been produced in response to a corporate-level (HQ) demand. In this case the strategy may have been written to satisfy corporate requirements, but it might not be adopted wholeheartedly by the business-level (SBU) team. Genuine ownership of the strategy by those responsible for implementing it is vital to its success.

Even where the team itself has agreed the strategy, there may be significant problems in implementation. The tendency towards maintaining the existing ways of doing things, and the resistance to change can be overwhelming. (This is explored further in Chapter 8.)

The 'Mission Statement' as a way of changing or setting the strategic direction of the business has, unfortunately, been devalued to some extent. This has happened where the Mission Statement is seen as a fashion item ('we must have one'), and where it consists of 'motherhood' statements* which no-one really believes can be acted upon.

Attempts deliberately to shape the strategy of the business may have foundered in the past either through weaknesses in the planning process itself, or through cynicism and a lack of ownership of the strategy amongst members of the top management team. Clearly, there is little point in drawing up a perfect competitive strategy if there is no chance of it being implemented.

Therefore, the process of determining the strategy needs to be one which generates the required levels of top team commitment. This usually means that the team itself should be responsible for coming up with the strategy, as involvement in the process usually generates commitment to the outcome. However, there is an additional process issue that must be recognized, where the top team is involved in the strategy process: the problem stems from the shared and common experiences of the team.

If the managers in the team all have similar experiences (perhaps they have worked in the same organization or the same industry for many years) then the way each manager sees the world, is likely to be quite similar. They are likely to share the same assumptions about, for example, the firm's strengths, about customers and their needs and about competitors. The problems stem from the fact that these shared assumptions are implicit. They are rarely made explicit, and hence are rarely debated or discussed. So, when the team discusses strategy, unless these assumptions are revealed and challenged in some way, they will inevitably influence the emerging strategy. These assumptions underpin the strategy debate.

The techniques and frameworks that are introduced in this book are there to help a team explore and challenge some of these implicit assumptions. The techniques we introduce should be used to broaden and deepen the strategy debate within the firm. In order to use some of these frameworks, new information will need to be

---

*A 'motherhood statement' implies a statement with which every reasonable person may be expected to agree. The state of motherhood is a virtuous one: hence 'we must put the customer first' is something of a motherhood statement.

generated, and issues that are not routinely discussed in management meetings will need to be addressed.

This book does not attempt to set out a foolproof process, or a set of checklists for strategy development. The ideas presented here need to be incorporated into an ongoing strategy process, and in this way the quality of the discussions should be enhanced.

The establishment of a competitive strategy should not be viewed as a yearly event, a ritual that has little impact on the reality of the organization. The strategy debate should be continuous – it should inform the agenda of top team meetings. Establishing a competitive strategy is the most important role of the top team at business unit level. This requires the intelligent management of the tensions between more routine operational issues, which may be urgent and important, but are essentially short term, and the longer-term development of sustainable competitive advantage.

These two aspects of top management activity must be integrated, because it is only through the transformation of routine operational activities that true competitive advantage is built. Competitive strategy can only be implemented through changes at the routine, operational level, so these two agendas, the short-term and the longer-term need to be creatively managed if competitive strategy is to be implemented.

1.3 Plan of the book

Delivering value to the customer is the cornerstone of competitive strategy. We therefore begin with an exploration of the Customer Matrix (Chapter 2). This simple device allows us to examine the basic strategy options that might be pursued by a firm with a given product in a selected market segment. It emphasizes that to gain sustainable competitive advantage the firm must deliver ever higher levels of Perceived Use Value (PUV) to customers at lowest Perceived Price.

In order to assess the relative effectiveness and efficiency of the firm, that is, its underlying core competences compared with those of its competitors, we employ the Producer Matrix (Chapter 3). The two matrices are designed to enable us to gain a depth of understanding about the following:

- The dimensions of perceived use value.

- Need-based segments of demand.
- The competitive positions of the firm's current products/services.
- The competences required to compete successfully.
- The relative cost positions of competitors.

Chapter 4 then considers how to assess the attractiveness of the competitive environment, and in particular to assess the relative individual strengths of competitors. Chapter 5 takes the analysis into the future, and into the realms of the real world of uncertain outcomes, building a model for the development of possible alternative scenarios. It enables us to ask questions such as: How might needs change? Will new firms be attracted into the market? Will demand in a segment increase or decrease? What broader environmental trends are likely to have an impact on the market, and how will they affect competition? Thus a picture emerges of the evolving competitive arena, which can then be used to help formulate a strategy.

Chapter 6 sets out a range of strategy options if acceptable performance cannot be predicted from continuing with the same product and market strategy. A simple system for evaluating alternative strategies is then described and applied.

To deliver the chosen strategy the firm has three alternatives:

- Joint development.
- Acquisition.
- Internal development.

Chapter 7 discusses some of the issues involved in the two higher-risk implementational strategies of finding an alliance partner for joint development, and acquiring a company in order to increase the firm's core competences.

Chapter 8 discusses some of the implications of implementing by internal development. In particular it concentrates on the issue of identifying blockages to change, and overcoming them by attempting to change some of the characteristics of the firm's culture to make it more closely aligned with the needs of the new strategy. Chapter 9 then provides the book with a brief synoptic conclusion, re-emphasizing the complementary roles of the Customer Matrix and the Producer Matrix in the process of competitive strategy development.

2

The Customer Matrix

Firms compete for customers, and competitive strategy is essentially about meeting the needs of customers more effectively than your competitors are able to meet them. In this chapter we introduce a simple device, the 'Customer Matrix' to explore issues in competitive strategy.

The vertical axis of Figure 2.1 ('Perceived Use Value') refers to the satisfaction experienced by the buyer in purchasing and using the product or the service. Perceived Use Value and Perceived Price represent the two components of 'value for money'. The Customer Matrix separates these out to assist us in analyzing competitive strategy. Perceived Price refers to the elements price that the customer is concerned with: for example, in purchasing a heating system for a house, the customer may not only be concerned with the initial cost of the installation (the price of the boiler, radiators, fittings, etc.) but may also be interested in the running costs of the system over the years (fuel costs, maintenance, etc.).

If a firm's product is positioned at point A in the chart, and the products of other firms perceived by the consumer to be alternative suppliers are positioned around point A (represented by the Xs in Figure 2.1), then as far as this consumer is concerned all the firms are offering equivalent products, and are charging very similar prices. This situation can be found in many industries, not just those that are supplying 'commodity' products, like coal or potatoes. In any circumstance where consumers perceive the products or services on offer to be more or less the same, the industry approximates to the circumstances depicted in Figure 2.1. This could be the case in, for example, the personal computer market, or in the choice of estate agencies.

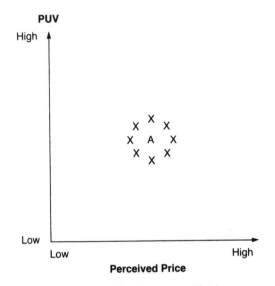

Figure 2.1   The Customer Matrix

If firm A is facing the situation depicted in Figure 2.1, what are the options available for improving its competitive position? As things now stand in the industry it is likely that all the firms will have a similar share of the market. So how can firm A improve its share? There are various moves that could be made in the chart that could improve the firm's competitive position: for example, the firm could cut price, or raise the PUV of the products or services it offers. These two basic strategic options will now be explored (see Figure 2.2).

2.1   Cutting price

Here the firm moves west in the Customer Matrix, offering the same Perceived Use Value as the competition, but at a lower price. Such a move should lead to firm A gaining share. However, this may depend on the type of products or services being offered. In some markets buyers perceive lower prices to mean lower Perceived Use Value. In other words, price is being used as an indirect way of measuring use value, where the customer reasons that 'If it's cheaper it can't be as good as the others.' If this was the situation facing firm A then a cut in price would move the firm to the

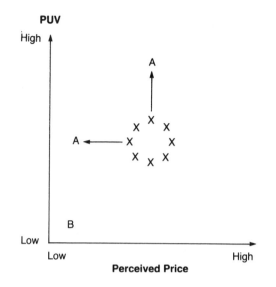

Figure 2.2 Basic competitive moves on the Customer Matrix

south-west, to a position offering lower Perceived Use Value at lower prices (position B in Figure 2.2). Managers need to be alert to this possibility. It often occurs when customers are unfamiliar with the purchase situation and they seek to reduce the riskiness of the purchase by using price as a proxy for value (e.g. when buying hi-fi equipment, dishwashers, perfume).

Let us assume that consumers are not using price as a proxy measure of Perceived Use Value, in which case the price cut moves firm A due west on the chart. This move should increase sales for firm A (and maybe in the industry as a whole if new customers are attracted into the market by the new lower prices). However, other firms are likely to respond to the move by cutting prices to match firm A's. The net result of the competitors' moving west with firm A is to reduce the average price and profitability of the industry.

Competitors can, then, imitate firm A's price-cutting strategy very rapidly. How, then, can firm A hope to gain sustainable competitive advantage from competing on price? Firm A must be able continually to drive down prices and sustain lower prices for a longer period than its competitors. This can only be achieved if firm A has either the lowest costs in the industry, or if the firm is able to sustain losses for extended periods, through subsidies from another part of the firm, or from the government.

If a firm is not the lowest-cost producer then the competitor with lower costs can always cut prices further, or sustain low prices for longer than firm A. To ensure that the firm is *the* lowest-cost producer it is necessary to be aware of the cost levels of competitors. Without cost information on competitors the management cannot be confident of achieving the lowest cost position, and this information is usually very difficult to obtain.

So if a firm chooses to compete on price it needs to have lower costs than its competitors. This involves exploiting all sources of cost reduction that do not affect Perceived Use Value (e.g. economies of scale, learning from experience, 'right first time' quality, just-in-time manufacturing). To be confident of achieving the lowest cost position the firm needs to have a clear picture of its own costs, and the costs of competitors. If a firm is able to achieve the lowest cost position it could choose to drive out competitors by sustaining very low prices. If, in the course of pursuing this strategy the firm is able to establish barriers to prevent other firms entering or re-entering the industry it could then opt to raise prices and hence profits, confident of its ability to defeat any potential entrants.

The risks of competing on price include the following:

- The firm may not be able to achieve the lowest costs in the industry. By definition only one firm can be in this position.
- The first firm to compete by cutting prices is likely to provoke its competitors into matching its lower price position as a defensive measure to protect market share. This could lead to a price war, with margins for all but the lowest cost players being cut to the bone.
- The emphasis on cost cutting encourages the management to focus inwards onto the internal operations of the firm. This may mean that little attention is focused on changing trends, tastes and competitive behaviour in the marketplace.

The last point can lead to a vicious circle for the firm. The inward orientation results in the firm lagging behind changing trends in the marketplace, and the firm's products are likely to become less competitive (they have lower Perceived Use Value than the competition). This forces the firm into competing on price, which reinforces the inward, cost-cutting orientation.

When markets are in decline (either temporarily due to recession, or permanently due to changing customer needs) firms may find themselves having to compete on price. But, as we have seen, unless a firm has low costs (preferably the lowest costs) it will inevitably struggle to stay profitable. This would suggest therefore that firms should aim to be low cost whether or not they intend to compete on price, because market conditions outside their control may at some point force them into price competition.

The firm needs to be lowest cost compared to those firms that the customer perceives to be alternative providers of Perceived Use Value. This may result in quite different definitions of competition from those typically made by managers, and they are likely to encompass fewer rather than more competitors. For example, if you are competing in the specialist sports-car market, you need to be low cost in relation to other existing or potential manufacturers of specialist sports cars, not in relation to producers of family saloons for the mass market.

2.2   Adding Perceived Use Value

The second basic strategy indicated in the Customer Matrix is the move north, gaining advantage through offering more Perceived Use Value for the same price as the competitors' products. The starting-point for this strategy must be the target customer, and the target customer's perception of value.

In order to effect this move north (rather than it resulting from luck, or trial and error), we must be clear about who our target customers are. We then must have a thorough understanding of their needs, and how they evaluate different product offerings. For example in choosing a new car, the customer may be interested in 'performance'. How is 'performance' evaluated? The importance of performance is also likely to vary from customer to customer, which suggests that there are different segments of demand, and the evaluation of performance will also vary. For some customers acceleration is critical, whereas for others it is top speed that counts.

This suggests that we need to cater for the individual customer. However, if we are confident that a substantial number of customers share similar needs, we can justifiably group these customers into a segment. So a segment is a group of customers with similar needs and perceptions of use value.

By systematically exploring customer needs and perceptions, through market research, and continually listening to customers, firms can discover what is valued in their products and services, and what could be added to them to improve PUV. Diagrams like Figure 2.3 can be constructed to establish the important dimensions of PUV

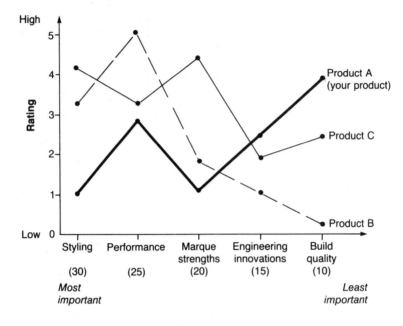

Figure 2.3 Dimensions of Perceived Use Value

for a particular segment. In this example of the luxury car market in Europe, the important dimensions of PUV include performance, styling and marque strength. The firm's products and those of its competitors are rated by consumers on each of these dimensions. It appears that this firm's car is seen to be inferior to the competition on the really important dimensions, but it performs well on the less-valued dimensions. If this firm is to move north on the Customer Matrix then either it has to shift significantly its customers' perceptions of its car's performance and styling, perhaps through an effective advertising campaign, or more ambitiously it might seek to shift customers' perceptions of the appropriate dimensions of use value. For example, it may be possible to persuade customers that engineering innovations and safety are more important than styling. Either way, unless the firm improves its position relative to the competition on these dimensions of Perceived Use Value, it will lag behind its competitors, leading to a below-average position on the Customer Matrix, and the firm may find itself forced to cut price to try to preserve sales levels.

2.3   What happens next?

The key issue facing firms pursuing a strategy of adding PUV is the ease with which competitors can match their moves. As a firm moves north on the matrix by adding PUV ahead of its competitors, it should be rewarded with an increased share of the market. The duration of the firm's enhanced position will depend on how easily the higher levels of PUV can be imitated. Over time it is likely that competitors will be able to match the move north, and the average level of PUV will be ratcheted upwards. Thus in most industries the minimum acceptable standards are being continuously shifted upwards as competitive moves are imitated; thus 'order-winning' features become 'order-qualifying' features. Air bags, for example, are now necessary just to remain in the executive car market, rather than helping to confer competitive advantage.

Thus the issue of sustainability of competitive advantage needs to be considered against this backdrop of continual northward shifts in the competitive arena. What can the innovator do once the competition has caught up? There are two basic options: **keep moving north** by staying one jump ahead of the competition through innovation or product enhancement; or **move west** through a cut in price. Perhaps the firm might do both at the same time, to effect an outpacing strategy.

We argued earlier that in order to compete on price, the firm needs to be the lowest cost producer in the market. So can you achieve the outpacing strategy of moving north to increase PUV and simultaneously achieve the lowest cost position? If the move north increases market share, and this translates into lower costs through scale and experience curve economies, then the move north would result in lower unit costs. Furthermore, if you understand what the customer really values you can confidently strip out everything that does not feed through to PUV. There is no point in offering a range of costly features if this is not what customers value. Of course if you are not confident about customers' real needs, then to play safe there is a tendency to leave everything in the product, because you are not sure which parts of the total package are the valued features.

It is clearly important to ensure that the cost of moving north does not exceed the added revenue from price and/or volume changes resulting from this move, otherwise a drop in profitability will result.

2.4   Other moves in the Customer Matrix

If the firm offers higher PUV, but demands a price premium for this added value, then this moves the firm's product position to the north-east on the matrix (see route 2 in Figure 2.4). The success of this strategy depends on the existence of a group of buyers who are prepared to pay higher prices for the added PUV. It also depends on the ease with which the increased PUV can be imitated. If imitation is easy then the price premium may be rapidly competed away.

A further problem with the move north-east is that it may well shift the product into a new up-market segment. For example, the new owners of an Italian restaurant may wish to move up-market. To achieve this they may introduce more exotic dishes onto the menu, dropping the more basic pasta and pizza main courses. An improvement of the décor follows, as does an increase of prices by 50 per cent. The price positioning of the restaurant will then be shifted away from the budget end of the market. However, compared with other up-market venues the restaurant's service levels, location, car parking and ambience may be perceived as inferior to the existing up-market venues. Bankruptcy may result, which may have been avoided if the restaurant had retained its original formula, which was well received in the budget segment of the market. However, it appears that other dimensions of value that

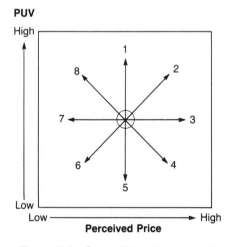

Figure 2.4   Competitive strategy options

the restaurant does not possess may clearly be important to customers in the higher-priced segment.

Route 3 on Figure 2.4 has the firm increasing price without adding any PUV. This move can succeed in increasing profitability, but only if competitors follow suit. For example, in the glass container industry in the early 1980s all firms were struggling for profitability, input costs were rising and firms did not feel able to pass these cost rises on to customers. Rockware made a unilateral move to increase price, which was followed by its major competitors. This resulted in the preservation of market shares and improved profits for the industry. If the Rockware move had not been followed by competitors making similar moves, Rockware would probably have lost market share. This move may happen after an interval of time following a price war that has pushed margins below the sustainable minimum for return on capital. But it can only do so if demand is strong enough to support the move. Incidentally, if consumers use price as a proxy measure for value, then a price increase may shift the firm onto route 2.

Route 4 (increasing price and decreasing value) is only feasible in a situation where there are supply constraints. Even then it is likely to lead to market disillusion, and can only be sustainable in the short term. It has been known to happen when management consulting firms increase their fees in line with inflation, but seek to boost profits by allocating junior consultants to a project and reducing the supervision time of more experienced seniors. In the longer term it is a route to decline and failure.

Route 5, reducing value but holding price constant, may come about inadvertently, either through attempts to cut costs, resulting in customers perceiving reductions in quality, or through competitors adding value, thereby causing a relative downward move in the firm's position on the PUV axis. It may also happen as in route 4 but without the double blow of the fee rise. Some of these moves can occur when the management is not clear about the dimensions of PUV, and how they are weighted by customers. Whatever the reasons, a move along route 5 is likely to result eventually in a reduction of market share.

Route 6, cutting price and PUV, is a diagonal move on the Customer Matrix which may well move the firm to a new, for them down-market, segment. For example, if a car manufacturer located in the middle ground of the car market, such as Ford, ventures along route 6 it will be signalling a change in competitors. Instead of competing with GM, Nissan and Renault it would now find itself compared with Lada, Proton or Skoda. This will only be a viable move if it does not reflect adversely on Ford's more up-market models, and if it has the cost structure to operate profitably against the low-priced competitors.

The only route that can be guaranteed to deliver an increased market share is route 8, increased PUV coupled with reduced price. However, to make this move and retain profitability, the firm must be the lowest-cost producer. It may have adopted a new low-cost technology, which has been the reason behind the price falls and PUV increases in many micro-chip based electronic goods in recent years. To sustain a move on route 8 the firm must be able to move faster than its competitors, as technological advance is normally soon copied. Often a firm will take route 1 initially, adding value, then when competitors imitate the added value, the firm will shift to route 7 by cutting price. The share advantage gained through the route 1 move should enable the firm to become the market leader through scale and experience economies, thus making the price-cutting strategy feasible. So the route 8 outcome may be achieved by following route 1 with route 7.

Route 8 is clearly a winning strategy as the product is perceived to be both cheaper and better than those of its rivals. However, all the other strategies involve balancing trade-offs between cheaper and better. Thus the process may be likened to a log-rolling competition with the log positioned diagonally on the axis between routes 2 and 6 (see Figure 2.5). Competitors try to convince the market that they are moving their part of the log in a north-westerly direction on the matrix, that is, offering higher PUV for a lower Perceived Price. They also try to create the impression that their competitors are falling off the log in the south-westerly direction, that is, offering less for higher prices. As soon as one competitor succeeds by general acceptance in moving north-west, this establishes a new position for the log. All parties to the south-east of it lose sales, and market competition resumes on the new axis.

As has been stressed, routes 2 and 6 may move the firm into serving different segments of demand. More generally, if a firm wishes to diversify into new markets the Customer Matrix should form part of the analysis. Before such a move is made management should ask the following questions:

- What do we know about customers in this segment? Specifically, what are their needs? What are the critical dimensions of PUV? What criteria do they use to evaluate products and services?

- What do we know about competitors? Who is here already? How are they positioned on the Customer Matrix?

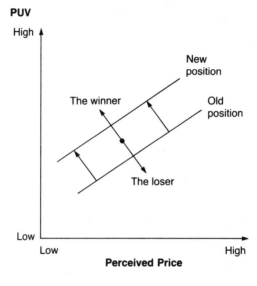

Figure 2.5 Log rolling

- Where should we try to enter the market?

The most critical question is: What makes us think that we can outperform the players who are already in this market? In addressing this question the management needs to explore the key competences firms need to compete successfully in this industry. This issue is discussed more fully in the next chapter.

2.5 Constructing the Customer Matrix

Although the principles behind competitive strategy are straightforward, achieving competitive advantage is intensely difficult. In trying to get to grips with the problems involved in crafting a competitive strategy, a structured approach to assessing a firm's competitive position should be adopted. In practising this approach it is recommended that initially a single segment of demand be analyzed. The analysis can then be extended to other target segments.

Step 1: identify segments

Buyer need is the appropriate basis for segmenting for the formulation of a competitive strategy. Thus one reasonably typical buyer should first be identified. This should be a real buyer, and not just a notional one. Then other potential buyers likely to have similar needs can be grouped with this representative buyer to form a segment. The process can then be repeated for other segments. Considerable judgement is needed to identify the point at which a given buyer belongs not to the segment being built, but to an adjoining one. Such judgement must rely upon the congruity or otherwise of the dimensions of Perceived Use Value in the segment.

Step 2: identify the PUV dimensions by segment

The dimensions of Perceived Use Value for a segment can only reliably be determined by asking customers what characteristics of a product they value. In carrying out this market research it is important not to present the customer with a list of product features. This will almost certainly confirm managers' preconceptions, rather than uncover something new and useful. It is important to understand the difference between the features of the product or service and the perceived needs of the buyer. From a basic understanding of needs, one can establish the relevant dimensions of value perceived by buyers in meeting these needs.

In the absence of access to the customer, the management team can brainstorm, using their collective experience to identify needs and use values. Such a process is, however, much less likely to reveal new insights than directly addressing customers.

Step 3: rate the dimensions of PUV

A large number of dimensions of PUV may have been generated by step 2. The next questions must be: Which are the most important, and how can weightings be applied? It is proposed that the five (say) most important dimensions be agreed on the basis of the customer survey, and 100 points be allocated across the five dimensions to represent weightings.

Step 4: assess firm's performance on the PUV axis

Once the most important and weighted dimensions of the PUV axis have been agreed the next step is to assess how well the firm currently performs with its current product in relation to the dimensions and in relation to its major competitors (see Figure 2.6). It may be necessary to rate all the competitors individually in relation to the dimensions before bringing them together on the matrix. Once more, if this is done too much in-house, without access to external data, great care must be taken to be neither too optimistic in relation to one's own performance nor indeed too pessimistic, if the culture of the company is to be constructively self-critical. Use of outsiders like industry analysts, customers or suppliers may provide a corrective mechanism in carrying out this step.

Step 5: plot positions on the matrix

The major competitors' positions on the matrix can now be plotted by combining the PUV analysis with the appropriate price information (see Figure 2.7). One check on the reliability of the ratings is to compare them with recent changes in relative market share. If one competitor is consistently getting high ratings on all critical dimensions of PUV, and is not known to have increased prices relative to other competitors, its market share would be expected to increase. If the market shares do not match the ratings a number of things may be wrong: the selected PUV dimensions, their weightings, the judgements of competitors' relative performance, or the market shares may well be lagged, for example in Figure 2.7 we would expect product B to be gaining share over our product A.

Step 6: identify PUV dimensions common across segments

The analysis of one segment may now be extended across other segments of demand. If there are common critical PUV dimensions, it should be possible to construct a competitive strategy which essentially addresses these core dimensions. This strategy should clearly set out the following:

- On which PUV dimensions the firm aims to be as good as the competition.
- On which PUV dimensions the firm aims to be better than the competition.

Dimension of PUV	Weighting	Product A (your product)		Product B		Product C	
	(Importance to customer)	Rating*	Rating × weight	Rating*	Rating × weight	Rating*	Rating × weight
Styling	30	1	30	3	90	4	120
Performance	25	3	75	5	125	3	75
Marque strength	20	1	20	2	40	4.5	90
Engineering innovations	15	2.5	25	1	15	2.0	30
Build quality	10	4	40	0.5	5	2.5	25
Total	100		190		275		340
Price			$20,000		$21,000		$26,500

Note: *Compared with your firm's product/service

Figure 2.6 Calculating PUV ratings for competitors' products

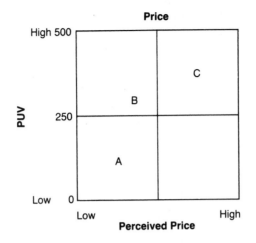

Figure 2.7 Plotting competitors' products on the Customer Matrix

Other dimensions of PUV that are peculiar to individual segments then need to be addressed, but the central thrust of the strategy could be built around the common core dimensions of PUV.

If there are few critical dimensions of PUV that are common across segments, then a multi-segment approach to competitive strategy may be necessary. The appropriate organizational form to address these different segments would probably be some form of Strategic Business Unit structure, which enables an SBU to focus relatively autonomously on a particular segment.

2.6 Summary

There are two basic ways in which a firm seeking competitive advantage can strengthen its position: by achieving greater PUV and by competing successfully on price. However, the only sustainably winning option is that which combines increased PUV with lower Perceived Price.

If the firm opts to compete on price alone it is vital that it has lower costs than its competitors. Otherwise it is likely that, if a price war develops, price levels will reach the point where the firm is forced out of business. In order to add PUV, it is essential to be clear who the target customers are, and what their needs are. On this understanding, the firm can develop approaches to adding Perceived Use Value in ways that are difficult to imitate.

Whether the firm is seeking to compete on price or to compete by adding PUV, it should strive to be the low-cost producer. The firm needs to be low cost compared to those firms the target customers perceive it to be in competition with. Achieving a low cost position through a strategy of adding Perceived Use Value is attainable if market share advantages enable the firm to realize the cost advantages accruing from scale and experience effects. Moreover, if the firm really understands what the customers value, then all costs that do not feed through to Perceived Use Value can be eliminated.

A move north-east (adding PUV and charging higher prices) or south-west (reducing both price and PUV) may involve a shift from one segment to another. Care needs to be taken to ensure that the firm can achieve a competitive advantage over the existing firms serving this segment.

In order to help management teams to construct the crucial tools described in Chapters 2 and 3, we have developed a software package using Windows™, which is available from the authors. The package enables you to construct all the key graphical tools explained in Chapters 3 and 4:

- The dimensions of PUV (Figure 2.3).
- The Customer Matrix (Figure 2.7).
- The Producer Matrix (Figure 3.1).
- The effectiveness competence profile (Figure 3.2).
- The cost efficiency competence profile (Figure 3.3).

In addition the software indicates the strategic issues and options associated with various combinations of positions in the Customer and Producer Matrices (as explained in Chapter 6).

3

The Producer Matrix

Throughout the 1980s, strategic thinking has been strongly influenced by Michael Porter's book *Competitive Strategy* (1980), in which market structure is said to play the greatest part in determining the profitability of a market. Within this approach the process of formulating a competitive strategy has been most commonly described as follows:

1. Analyze the environment for attractive industry segments.
2. Identify, evaluate and select the appropriate strategies for competing in the chosen industry segments: low cost, differentiation or focus.
3. Implement the chosen strategy.

The thinking behind this process is that the attractiveness of the industry is the prime determinant of profitability. However, there is evidence (see Rumelt 1991) to show that variation of profit levels in firms within industries is at least as great as that between industries. Furthermore, the undoubted profit record of the Hanson Group and others, the fundamental strategy of which frequently involves investing in apparently unattractive industries but running companies efficiently, casts further doubt on this emphasis.

It can also lead a firm that believes it has identified an attractive opportunity, such as cable television, to embark on an investment in that opportunity area, without paying sufficient attention to the question of whether running a cable television company actually builds upon something the firm has experience in doing well, and in which it can therefore reasonably expect to have some competitive advantage.

Whilst any strategist would probably concede the strategy process can only be carried out by an examination of both the external environment and the internal strengths of the firm, the emphasis placed upon the sequence in which this exercise is carried out is important.

The resource-based theory of competitive advantage suggests that competitive advantage is best sought by an examination first of a firm's existing resources and core competences; then an assessment of their profit potential in relation to the congruent opportunities presented by the market, and the selection of strategies based upon the possibilities this reveals. The task is then to fill whatever resource or competence gap is identified by the inventory taking of existing resources and competences, in relation to the perceived profit potential of a given opportunity. From this analysis emerges a set of decisions to build competences internally, to form alliances with other firms with complementary competences or to acquire a firm with such competences. This book will deal with all three options (see Chapters 6 and 7).

This process would discourage a firm from investing in an enterprise that was not strongly related to its competences. Only strategies based upon existing competences could, it would hold, lead to the acquisition and maintenance of sustainable competitive advantage. Thus a would-be athlete wondering what event to specialize in would be more likely to succeed by considering his qualities first before considering the attractiveness of the event. If he is 5 foot 6 inches in height and weighs 200 pounds, neither the high jump nor the marathon seem likely events in which he might expect to excel, however hard he trains. By selecting throwing the hammer or the javelin, however, he might well, given training and technique, achieve eminence. Similarly, a company is only likely to excel in areas where it is already highly competent, and for which a strategic opportunity has arisen. If it lacks the basic core competences, it may become acceptably proficient, but is unlikely to achieve competitive advantage.

In contrast to the market structure view of profit potential, the resource-based theory suggests that above-average profits arise in a firm because it is able to make use of certain core resources and competences better than its competitors, and because these competences mesh better with the current key competences required for success in the industry than do those of its rivals.

The market structure approach assumes the ultimate arrival in markets of 'normal' conditions of equilibrium (i.e. a balance of supply and demand at a price acceptable to both buyers and sellers) in which above-average profits will have been competed away, and appropriate rational strategies will have led to the end-game of a commodity product produced by a small number of the most efficient firms each with low costs and minimal differentiation. Indeed some industries do display these characteristics, such as the personal computer hardware industry, but by no means all do so, and generally not those in which sustainable long-run profits are to be made.

The resource-based approach, however, has a radically different view of likely outcomes. By contrast with the market structure approach, it assumes a state of disequilibrium as the norm; that firms differ essentially from each other for reasons of history, of differing asset endowments both inanimate and human, and through the development of distinct capabilities. At given moments in time, industries will display characteristics that make certain factors key to superior profitability for firms possessing them. The firms able to achieve above-average profits will be those whose competences match most closely the key strategic industry factors. These competences may be called the firms' strategic assets. However, they need to be deployed with an appropriate strategy in order to capitalize on the above-average profits available.

Unfortunately managers have only 'bounded rationality' and are frequently faced with conditions of high uncertainty and complexity. They also face the problem of resolving potential organizational conflict within the firm arising from the differing personal agendas and ambitions of the firm's executives. The selection and implementation of the most profitable strategy, even by firms possessing the core competences most appropriate in relation to the industry's key requirements, is therefore fraught with risk and limited probability of a successful outcome. The supposed predictability in terms of market evolution of the market-based theory, developed from classical economic theory, is thus replaced by the strategic uncertainty of firms, even with the most appropriate core competences, groping in the fog of uncertain futures. Such a description of the 'real' world is not without credibility. However, even with these limitations to the probability of success, if the game is to be played, the search must be made for the most valued core competences, and for the key to how to use them most profitably.

3.1   The nature of the Producer Matrix

Using this resource-based perspective, the problem posed for the strategist is how to achieve a sustainable and superior position on the Customer Matrix described in Chapter 2 above, through the appropriate use and development of the firm's core competences. The matrix in Figure 3.1, which we may call the Producer Matrix, illustrates the relationship between relative unit cost and key value-creating competences (effectiveness) that the strategist must try to manipulate in order to improve the firm's position on the Customer Matrix for a particular market. The competences on the vertical axis may be called the effectiveness competences as they are most concerned with enhancing value. The horizontal axis refers to the relative unit cost position of the competing firms.

The competences on the vertical axis of the Producer Matrix must translate through to PUV on the Customer Matrix for them to bring about genuine sustainable competitive advantage. Secondly, they must be superior to those of close competitors on the Producer Matrix. If the firm improves its core competences, but competitors improve their equivalent competences even more, the firm will go down, not up the vertical axis, and will become less competitive.

Thus an understanding of the two matrices is vital to achieving competitive advantage, since their linkage is indirect. Competitive advantage can only be achieved as a result of movement on the Customer Matrix, since that advantage comes at a point of resolu-

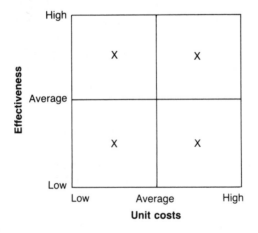

Figure 3.1   The Producer Matrix

tion between the buyer's perception of use value and of price. Yet the firm can only act directly on its Producer Matrix either by increasing its core competences in order to attempt to increase PUV, or by lowering its costs through improving efficiency to put itself in a position to exercise flexibility on price. Competitive advantage is a customer-determined characteristic, and the actions of the producer can at best attempt to achieve it uncertainly through movements in the Producer Matrix.

Situations also exist, however, where the Customer Matrix and the Producer Matrix may not be in harmony; for example:

1. Improvements in core competences may lead to a move north-wards above the horizontal in the Producer Matrix. However, this could result in movement north or south or no movement at all on the PUV axis of the Customer Matrix as the would-be customer reacts positively, negatively or not at all to the firm's attempt to improve PUV. So unless the enhanced levels of competence result in improvements perceivable to the customer, no shift occurs on the Customer Matrix.

2. A shift northwards on the Customer Matrix may come about spontaneously due to a change in public tastes, without any core competence improvement at all.

3. The firm may move westward on the Producer Matrix by reducing its costs, but may judge that market conditions suggest a supply constraint, and may thus opt to increase its margins by raising prices; thus causing an eastward move on the Customer Matrix.

4. Despite a westward move on the Producer Matrix, the firm may equally well choose to keep price the same, raise it or lower it. However, without a significant westward move on the Producer Matrix, it is unlikely to have the freedom to bring about a westward move on the Customer Matrix.

3.2 Determining the core competences

How then does a firm determine what are its core competences? These divide into two categories:

1. Operational competences.
2. System competences.

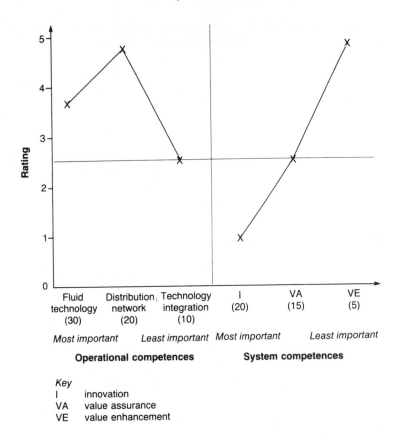

Figure 3.2 Competitive profile: effectiveness for printing inks industry

Operational competences are the specific 'technical' competences that are relevant to operating in a particular market. In Figure 3.2 the key operational competences for this firm in the printing technology industry are fluid technology, distribution and technology integration.

A firm's 'effectiveness' as opposed to its cost efficiency may be strongly influenced by its operational competences.

System competences typically span the range of core activities performed by the firm. They may be as great a source of competitive advantage as its more easily defined operational competences, and cover both effectiveness and cost efficiency aspects of the firm.

Generic effectiveness systems competences include the following:

1. Value assurance.
2. Value enhancement.
3. Innovation.

These are discussed below.

1. Value assurance is the effectiveness process that ensures that constant cost reduction does not lead to concomitant value loss, with the inevitable result of declining PUV. Value assurance takes as its watchword that it is cheaper to get a product right first time than to have to reprocess it to correct faults. A zero defect policy is therefore a critically important one for a firm aiming to maximize its value assurance competence. Such an attitude is not restricted to a firm's products, but applies equally to its corporate philosophy, and hence overall and detailed methods of working and managing. Value assurance can apply as much to the competence with which meetings are run as to the quality of a product produced. Value or quality assurance has been at the forefront of innovations in the way firms are managed. This is partly because it helps a firm improve both its effectiveness (the products are more consistent and reliable) and its cost efficiency (less scrap and reworking means lower unit costs).

2. Value enhancement covers the processes whereby existing products or services are constantly reviewed with the aim of upgrading them, and enhancing their level of PUV. Each constituent dimension of PUV should be regularly monitored, and checked for possible change, and the product offering reviewed to match it ever more closely to that PUV by the perpetual development of the core competence activities and processes that lead to such enhancement.

3. Innovation is a competence present in some companies in high measure, but quite absent from others. Some measure of a company's innovatory capacity can be measured by calculating what proportion of its sales turnover is provided by products internally developed over the last five years. Whereas some companies rely strongly on the regular up-dating of existing products (e.g. IBM), others (e.g. Sony) seem able to develop totally new products on a regular basis. These latter are the innovatory companies. It should be noted that high innovatory activity is closely correlated with high risk, as totally new products typically have a high failure rate. Figure 3.3 below similarly describes the cost competences.

We will now explore the generic systems competences relating to limit costs in more detail starting with the cost efficiency competence of continual cost reduction. (See Figure 3.3 below.)

In order to achieve low unit costs the firm needs to develop efficiency capabilities and competences. These can be classified into four generic areas of competence:

4. Continual cost reduction.
5. Economies of scale and scope.
6. Control and coordination.
7. Factor costs.

4. Continual cost reduction processes involve the firm developing a corporate mind-set that is the opposite of that naturally found in organizations. The 'natural' tendency of organizations is to grow in numbers as they find reasons to justify extra support or information functions, and to develop product variants to meet an increasing number of special needs. To reverse this tendency the firm needs to adopt processes that continually strive towards design simplification, and organizational simplification. Nissan, for example, are said to aim to take 10 per cent out of their costs of production of a model each year. When this proves no longer possible, it is the signal for the next generation of product to take over. The learning or experience curve is a representation of the cost advantages that can accrue if a firm is dedicated to continual cost reduction.

5. Economies of scale and scope. Scale economies can come about, for example, as a result of capital investment, such that larger volume leads to equipment being used more intensively and hence lowers costs per unit. Scope economies relate to the economies achieved through more intensive use of a function, for example a brand name or a sales force. These effects reduce the unit cost of an activity and thus increase the possibility of it achieving competitive advantage.

6. Control and coordination describe the processes that enable the firm to operate collectively in an optimally efficient way. It is frequently this set of processes that distinguish the sustainably competitive company from its less well-run competitors. It is often the nature of the control and coordination functions that creates difficult-to-imitate levels of efficiency in certain companies: competitors can analyze what the excellent companies do, but they find it

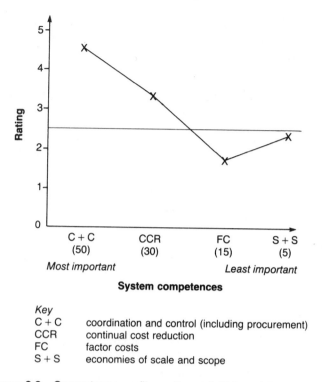

Figure 3.3 Key
C + C   coordination and control (including procurement)
CCR   continual cost reduction
FC   factor costs
S + S   economies of scale and scope

Figure 3.3 Competence profile: unit cost (efficiency) for all industries

impossible to get similar high-quality results from imitating their methods. Effective coordination across the range of the firm's activities reduces wastage and work in progress, and speeds up cycle times. Techniques like just-in-time manufacturing assist in improving coordination; but effective coordination also extends beyond the firm to include links with other parts of the corporation (e.g. with a centralized procurement activity) and links with suppliers and customers.

7. **Factor costs** include the cost of labour, power, land, buildings and capital. Some firms that are located in developing countries may have considerable factor cost advantages which enable them to be very low cost, even though their other system competences, such as continual cost reduction, may be relatively weak. Moreover, firms in high factor cost locations may need to compensate for these cost disadvantages by developing excellence in other system competences, such as value assurance.

We now consider the generic system competences associated with improving the effectiveness of the firm, that is, enhancing its ability to deliver PUV.

3.3   Sustainable competitive advantage

What characteristics does a core competence matched to a market opportunity possess? Clearly, it must have distinctive qualities that earn above-average profits over the longer term, and thus must be difficult to imitate. Grant (1991) suggests that to sustain competitive advantage strategic resources and competences need to score well when screened for four characteristics, namely:

1. Appropriability.
2. Durability.
3. Transferability.
4. Replicability.

We will discuss each in turn, since the key task of the strategist in internal analysis is to identify the firm's key strategic resources and competences that seem to have high potential sources of sustainable competitive advantage, and to screen them against the four defining dimensions of sustainability.

1.   **Appropriability.** This is concerned with the degree to which the profits earned by a particular strategic asset can be appropriated by someone other than the firm in which the profits were earned. The lower the appropriability of the asset the more it may be able to sustain profits for the firm. An asset is difficult to appropriate if it is deeply embedded in the firm, and the firm can easily sustain the loss, for example, of a high-performing executive to a competitor. The problem arises because of the fact that firms own fixed assets, but not the skills of individuals. Thus, for example, if in a football team a star emerges with high goal-scoring ability, he owns that skill and is empowered either to take it to a competitor, or to use it to gain in salary or other benefits, a high percentage of the profits from the owners of the team he represents. Similarly, certain film stars are able to appropriate to themselves a substantial percentage of the profits of films in which they appear, as they are able to convince the films' producers that without their star name the profits would not be achieved. In the business world certain well-known chief executives of major corporations are similarly successful in appropriating high compensation to themselves with these arguments.

If, however, the profits can confidently be ascribed to the routines and team excellence developed by a wide range of managers and staff within the company, then the profits cannot be so appropriated, as the loss of any individual will not be perceived as affecting profits to any large extent. When a firm has been performing excellently over a period of time, the competence may even transcend individuals or teams, and become a competence of the firm itself in an 'organizational learning' way. Low appropriability of the strategic asset therefore means high profit sustainability.

2. Durability. This characteristic of a strategic asset applies not so much to its physical durability as to its durability as a source of profit. The more intangible aspects of durability are therefore more important here. Shortening product and technology life cycles make most assets less durable than they were even a decade earlier.

However, if tangible assets are proving to have declining durability as sources of sustainable profits, the more intangible distinguishing characteristics of firms are not suffering in this regard. Firms' routines, core competences and team methods can and do survive passing generations of products. Firms' reputations do not decay with the years so long as they do not visibly decline in their essential perceived innovative, productive and high-quality characteristics. Similarly, leading brand names prove remarkably durable. As products come and go such household names as Kellogg's, Nestlé, Du Pont and Xerox continue with undimmed reputations in the public's eyes. Any one of these can, however, all too easily prove to have reputations of perishable durability, given no more than a year of poor performance. The recent diminishing reputation of IBM is a salutary illustration of this. However, the more durable the core competence clearly the higher the profit sustainability.

3. Transferability. The easier it is to transfer the core competences and resources, the lower the sustainability of their competitive advantage. Some resources are obviously easy to transfer, for example raw materials, employees with standard skills, machines and to some extent factories, where the transferability may be through change of ownership rather than physical transportation. In this sense such assets are not strategic, due to the ease with which they can be bought and sold. Once more the essential characteristic of a strategic asset is the degree to which it is firm-specific, embedded within the fabric of the firm, within its culture and its mode of operation. Such capabilities represent the profit-sustaining assets of the firm. The less transferable these assets the greater their strategic profit-sustaining quality.

4. Replicability. If the competence or resource cannot easily be transferred, it may be possible, by appropriate investment or simply by purchasing similar assets for a competitor, to construct a nearly identical set of capabilities. If this is possible, the original firm possessed no real durable competitive advantage. The economist's equilibrium theory will operate here, and a profitable company will find its profits competed away, as new entrants replicate its resources and competences and produce similar products, thereby reducing price through competition and moving the product inexorably towards commodity low-profit status. The easier the replicability, the lower the strategic importance of the resources and competences in question.

Core competences that qualify as strategic assets with profit-sustaining capacity then, need to have high durability, and low appropriability, transferability and replicability.

3.4   Filling resource and skill gaps

The four qualities sought in a core competence all point to the requirement that the asset, resource or competence be something intangibly unique to the company possessing it. It cannot easily be appropriated, made obsolete, transferred or replicated. It is not easily imitable.

The operations and systems that a firm performs up to the best in the industry are described as its core competences. These may not entirely mesh with the competences required to achieve sustainable competitive advantage in a particular market. Those competences required for this purpose are described as key competences, and will vary from market to market. In the event of a firm's core competences not matching its key or required competences, the firm must seek to acquire the additional resources or competences by internal development, by strategic alliance or by acquisition. The caveat here, however, is that the sought-after resources must be only a small proportion of the existing resources, or the risk exists that the newly acquired competences will so outbalance the existing ones as to change the nature of the firm, and thereby reduce the effectiveness of the existing competences. So long as the acquired competences are restricted to this small proportion of the whole, the firm can continue to develop its competences effectively and incrementally.

Thus a firm, or in an alliance more than one firm, seeks to develop a range of core competences that potentially enable it to match the key competences necessary to succeed in its chosen markets.

3.5   Constructing the Producer Matrix

In constructing the Producer Matrix the management team will probably discover that the firm lacks adequate information about competitors. It is suggested that for a 'first pass' the matrix should be constructed based on the collective experience of the team. The following structured approach should be taken.

Step 1: prepare an activity cost chain analysis

It is generally helpful to prepare some form of activity cost or value chain analysis of the product/market under review. This involves plotting the activities that take the product from its raw material state within the company, which could be in the form of bought-in components, through the manufacturing stage, if appropriate, and on to after-sales service. In each of these activities costs can be noted and the key characteristics of the activity carried out. This clarifies what the firm actually does to get the product onto the market, and may then give insights into how the process could be improved. Figure 3.4 illustrates the activity chain of a power services manufacturer in producing standard back-up generator sets. The analysis clearly reveals that the company adds little value (effectiveness competences), since 85 per cent of total cost is bought in. It also notes the high level of maturity of the market. It does not therefore take much insight to realize that the product is largely a commodity one, and that therefore the cost efficiency competences will be the ones crucial to success.

Step 2: agree segment definition

It is important to be very specific about the market segment being addressed, since different competences with different weightings will be applicable for different segments. As with the Customer Matrix, it may be possible to develop a more generic matrix of the company's competences at a later stage. This will be useful when judgements are being made on which new segments to enter.

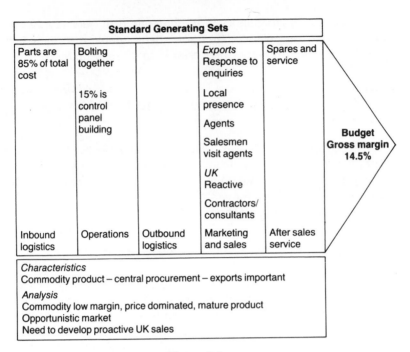

Figure 3.4

Step 3: identify key operational and system competences

The firm's management team needs to answer the question: What does a firm need to be really excellent at, in order to win in this segment? For example, in the corporate banking sector an individual competitor may need key operational skills in dealing, market making, lending and investment. It may also need a strong reputation, track record and strong balance sheet. It will need to highlight which of the systems competences are really critical to success, for example value assurance, value enhancement and so forth, and these should be identified and weighted as for the Customer Matrix.

Step 4: rate the firm's competences against those of key competitors

The firm's management team need now to conduct a similar exercise for the firm's key competitors and to relate them to each other so that they can be plotted on the vertical axis of the Producer Matrix. If some relative cost information is available it may be possible to locate competitors on the horizontal 'unit cost' axis. If direct information on competitive costs is difficult to access, an estimate of relative costs could be derived from exploring the system competences associated with cost efficiency, such as continual cost reduction, economies of scale and scope, coordination and control, and factor costs. Informed, albeit subjective, assessments should enable the team to construct a cost efficiency competence profile as in Figure 3.3. The scores and weightings can then be used to locate competitors on the horizontal axis of the Producer Matrix.

Step 5: develop a core competences matrix across segments

Once more, as with the Customer Matrix, the Producer Matrices by segment should be inspected to identify the most common key competences that are required across segments within the industry, as this is likely to give a clear view of the firm's fundamental core competences and indeed incompetences. Using the approaches described above, it should be possible for a management team to construct a set of Customer and Producer Matrices for the major market segments it is currently operating within.

To recapitulate: the Customer Matrix will show how the firm's product is positioned against those of competitors on the two dimensions, Perceived Use Value and Perceived Price. The Producer Matrix will indicate the firm's position relative to its competitors on the dimensions of effectiveness and cost efficiency. The positioning on the Producer Matrix is arrived at through a consideration of the operational competences required to deliver PUV, and the relative importance of the various system competences, that is, those concerned with effectiveness – value assurance, value enhancement and innovation – and those concerned with efficiency – continual cost reduction, economies of scale and scope, overall coordination and control, and factor costs. Appropriate weighting of the competences may be necessary to produce an accurate assessment, since the importance of particular competences varies from segment to segment.

The Customer Matrix indicates the current situation in a particular product/market. The Producer Matrix, being a firm-level device, reflects the relative situation with regard to competences that are required to compete in this product market. In practice the same (or very similar) competences may be required in a number of different but related product markets. For example, in the insurance industry competences in systems, underwriting, managing relationships with brokers and with re-insurers may be required in most insurance product markets.

Because the Producer Matrix reflects the relative positions of the firm's competences in relation to its rivals, it can provide some indication of how competitors may be able to manoeuvre on the Customer Matrix in the future. For example, a firm may have been building its core competences to achieve a strong relative position on the Producer Matrix, which may enable it to move aggressively on the Customer Matrix. In this sense, the Customer Matrix reflects the situation today, whereas the Producer Matrix provides indications of how the Customer Matrix may evolve in the future.

3.6 Summary

The market attractiveness theory suggests that all major possibilities for profit emerge from the market. The key to success is therefore to identify an attractive area to compete in. The resource-based theory, in contrast, hands the power for winning above-average profits to the firm, and its ability to develop unique inimitable competences that it can profitably direct to an appropriate market.

This chapter argues that both the market and the resource sides of the equation are relevant to the achievement of sustainable competitive advantage. However, it suggests that the development of a unique firm-specific and deeply embedded set of core competences matched to a market opportunity is more likely to lead to sustainable competitive advantage and above-average profits than a strategic approach that concentrates primarily on identifying a market need and then sets out to meet it, without concern for the need to develop capabilities in the firm over time.

The construction of a Producer Matrix with axes of effectiveness and cost efficiency provides a producer's mirror on the internal company side to reflect, in successful cases, the market-determined Customer Matrix on which ultimately sustainable competitive advantage is measured.

4

The competitive environment

In his book, *Competitive Strategy* (1980), Michael Porter develops a useful framework for analyzing the structure of an industry or market segment, from the viewpoint of its attractiveness to a player already in the industry. For the purposes of this analysis an industry is defined as a group of firms producing similar goods or services for the same market. Porter's approach concentrates on the competitive forces operating in the industry, the outcome of the analysis being an assessment of the attractiveness of the industry, defined by how profitable the industry is for the firms already in it. The real benefit of the approach is that it forces the management team to view the industry from a broader perspective than would typically be the case. The discipline of assessing the relative strengths of the forces operating in the industry can develop new and important insights into the competitive environment, which can help in the construction of better competitive strategies.

Porter argues that there are five competitive forces which operate in an industry and together determine the potential profitability of that industry. The five forces are as follows:

- Rivalry amongst existing firms.
- The barriers to new entrants.
- The bargaining power of buyers.
- The bargaining power of suppliers.
- The threat from substitute products or services.

Each will be considered in turn. Figure 4.1 sets out a schematic checklist of the forces.

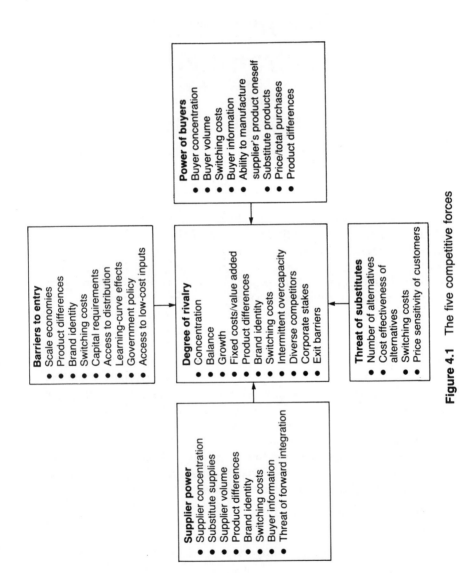

Figure 4.1 The five competitive forces

4.1   Rivalry

Rivalry refers to the intensity of competitive behaviour within the industry. It addresses such issues as whether firms are continually seeking to outmanoeuvre their rivals through price cuts, new product innovations, advertising, credit deals or promotional campaigns. Or perhaps there is little competitive activity, firms being content to stick with their shares of the market, and being unwilling to upset the balance of the industry by, say, instigating a price war. There are a number of factors which, Porter suggests, determine the probable intensity of rivalry in an industry.

- **Slow growth of or declining demand.** If demand slows, firms can only maintain historic growth rates by gaining market share from competitors. This tends to intensify rivalry as firms battle for share by price cuts or other attempts to boost sales. Declining demand will lead to further intensification of competitive activity, particularly if there are exit barriers to the industry. These barriers can take the form of large investments of capital that has no alternative use, few transferable skills, and high costs of plant closure including redundancy costs.

- **High fixed costs.** If the cost structure of the industry is such that there is a high fixed cost, and low marginal cost component, then firms will be under intense pressure to produce near full capacity. So if demand falls off, firms will use price cuts and other weapons to maintain sales. Similar behaviour can occur in industries with highly perishable products.

- **Unpredictable and diverse competitors.** If the industry is made up of a diverse group of firms, their behaviour is likely to be unpredictable. If there are new entrants from other countries or industries that do not play by the 'rules' their maverick behaviour is likely to lead to an extremely volatile competitive arena.

- **Low switching costs.** Switching costs are costs incurred by the buyer in moving from one supplier to another. For example switching costs are incurred if an airline moves from an all Boeing fleet to a mixed Airbus/Boeing fleet, such as the need for crew training, spares inventories and so forth. If switching costs are low in an industry, buyers are able to switch between suppliers without any penalty. Switching costs may be tangible as in the airline example, or may be composed of the intangible costs of being accustomed to working smoothly with a particular supplier.

● **A commodity product.** The more a firm is able to differentiate its product either by establishing a strong brand name, or offering clearly distinct PUV, the less it needs to fear its rivals, as it is laying claim to the argument that it alone supplies a given market need. Correspondingly the nearer its product is to being a commodity the greater is likely to be the rivalry it faces. Brand names therefore tend to reduce rivalry since they emphasize differentiation, and establish at least psychological switching costs for the consumer if he/she is to move to a different brand.

● **Cyclicality leading to periodic overcapacity.** During these periods of spare capacity rivalry will be intense as firms fight to fill their factories.

● **High corporate stakes.** In difficult times the options are 'fight or flight'. If the market is an important one to the main players in it they will be inclined to fight. This will also be the case if exit costs are high.

4.2   Barriers to entry

If new firms enter an industry they bring additional capacity. If demand is not increasing to absorb this additional capacity, then the new entrants will have to compete for a share of the existing demand. To gain entry they may either compete with lower prices or with enhanced product features or both. The net effect of these new entrants will probably be to lower the overall level of profitability in the industry. Entry is deterred by the presence of barriers, which can stem from a number of sources.

● **Economies of scale.** If there are major cost advantages to be gained from operating at a large scale then new entrants will either have to match that scale or have higher unit costs, and suffer lower margins. Scale economies are usually thought of as a production phenomenon, but may also exist in advertising, purchasing, R&D and after-sales services and elsewhere.

- **Experience benefits.** Low unit costs can be achieved by accumulated learning, that is, finding progressively more efficient ways of doing things, which if they are significant would place by definition inexperienced new entrants at a unit cost disadvantage.

- **Access to know-how.** Patents can protect firms from new entrants, and access to process knowledge and particular skills can make entry difficult.

- **Customer brand loyalty.** Customers may have preferred brands, or they may have strong relationships with their existing suppliers, which they are reluctant to break. New entrants would have to persuade customers that it was worth their while incurring these switching costs involved in moving to the product of a new entrant. This may provide a strong barrier to entry.

- **Capital costs of entry.** If capital costs are high this will limit the number of potential entrants. Such costs include setting up production facilities, research and development costs, establishing dealer networks and initial promotion expenses.

- **Access to distribution channels.** It would be difficult for an unknown player to persuade the major grocery retailers to take its products without substantial inducements of some sort, possibly a large advertising support campaign. If all major distribution outlets are already closed to the new entrant they may be faced with the added expenditure of setting up their own direct distribution network.

- **High switching costs.** If customers will incur high switching costs if they move to a new entrant's product, this constitutes a barrier to entry. Thus if IBM have a high installed base in the mainframe computer market this constitutes a very effective barrier to the entry of other potential rivals, as winning orders against the supplier of the installed base would require a really special advantage to overcome the switching costs of changing computer systems.

- **Government policy** may also provide a barrier to entry as the government seeks to regulate the industry by restricting licences, issuing exclusive franchises or establishing regulations that are onerous and costly to implement.

- **Access to low-cost inputs** may also provide a barrier to entry by potential competitors without such access. Low labour costs in the Far East thus have provided barriers to the development of, for example, textile industries in the developed world.

4.3 The bargaining power of buyers

Buyers or customers can have considerable bargaining power for a variety of reasons:

- When there are few buyers, and they purchase in large quantities.
- When the buyers have low switching costs, and therefore probably low loyalty. Thus highly differentiated products offer less opportunity for the exercise of buyer power than do relatively undifferentiated products.
- When buyers face many relatively small sellers.
- When the item being purchased is not an important one for the buyer, and therefore he/she can take it or leave it.
- When they have a lot of information concerning competitive offers, which they can use for bargaining.
- When there is a real risk that the buyer may decide to integrate backwards, i.e. to make the product itself rather than buy it in.

Examples of powerful buyers include Marks and Spencer, with their many relatively small clothing suppliers, and the Ministry of Defence, with suppliers of military equipment. Here buying power is highly concentrated, and failure to win an order can have severe implications for a firm's survival.

More generally, where buyers are faced with many alternatives and the cost of switching is low or non-existent, buyers have power. The more concentrated the buyers the greater the power. Buyer power is normally evidenced by the ability of the buyer to bargain the price downwards.

4.4 The bargaining power of suppliers

Correspondingly the ability of suppliers to increase prices without losing sales illustrates their power. Such power may come about in the following circumstances:

- The purchase is important to the buyer.
- Buyers have high switching costs.
- There are few alternative sources of supply.
- Any particular buyer is not an important customer of the supplier.
- There is the real risk that the supplier may integrate forward: e.g. instead of the car maker supplying its independent dealers, it may decide to set up its own dealer subsidiary.

Examples of powerful supplier relationships would be gas supply to the glass container industry, and micro-chip suppliers to the computer industry. The term 'suppliers' includes the providers of capital and of specialist skills. Thus if an industry is dependent on particularly skilled people, these individuals can bargain up their pay levels; for instance, advertising agencies are highly dependent on a few creative individuals and their pay is accordingly high.

If suppliers are powerful they can increase the prices of their inputs, thus extracting potential profits from the industry. If firms are facing powerful suppliers and buyers profits will be severely squeezed, as input cost increases cannot be passed on in higher prices to buyers. Such a situation is likely to make the industry unattractive to potential entrants.

4.5   The threat of substitutes

Industries are usually defined in terms of the products or services they provide. Thus we have the aluminium can industry, the sugar industry or the pizza restaurant industry. This enables us to identify a group of firms doing similar things who are in competition with each other. However, if we define industries from the buyer's perspective, we might come up with a quite different set of firms, who do not provide similar products, but who do nevertheless meet the same type of buyer needs. The buyer who likes sweet coffee might consider manufacturers of sugar and of artificial sweeteners to be in direct competition. A lunchtime shopper may see a pizza restaurant, a hamburger outlet, a pub and a delicatessen selling sandwiches as being in direct competition for his/her custom.

Substitute products are alternative ways of meeting buyer needs. In this way the fax machine provides a substitute for the letter but not for parcel post. The effect of substitute products on the previously product-defined industry is to place a ceiling on prices, since a price rise may cause a previously loyal customer to shift to the substitute product. In this regard no purchase at all may have the same effect as that of a substitute product, as both represent a reduction of effective demand from the industry.

Defining the boundaries of an industry is more an art than a science, and is crucial to an accurate assessment of industry attractiveness. If too narrow a product-based definition is adopted there are risks that the analysis will miss critical aspects of the competitive environment. Some industries are geographically fragmented, with each locality having just one or two producers, for example quarries, cinemas, zoos or regional newspapers. In most respects such firms in different regions are not direct competitors. Therefore one of the key decisions to make in a five-force analysis is the choice of industry boundary. The market is not an arbitrary one, it is a 'strategic market', that is, one supplying a distinct customer-determined need to a geographically defined customer group. Whether it be local, regional, national, pan-national (e.g. the European Community) or global, the characteristics of the market will determine which of these types of market is appropriate for a particular analysis. Thus although the corrugated cardboard market is said to be limited to a fifty-mile radius of the producer for reasons of transport costs in relation to an undifferentiated product, the market for video-recorders can be legitimately regarded as global. The five-force analysis boundaries adopted must reflect these different facts if the analysis is to be useful for generating insights into possible competitive strategies.

The threat of substitutes is high in the following circumstances:

- There are a number of equally cost-effective ways of meeting the same customer need.
- The customer faces few switching costs in moving to the substitute product.
- The customer exhibits high price sensitivity, and the substitute is a low-price one.

4.6 The advantages of the five-force framework

The main benefit of using this technique is that it provides a structure for management thinking about the competitive environment. Each force can be examined using the checklist set out above. Some aspects will be highly relevant to the industry and some less relevant. Some useful insights into the nature of the industry will usually emerge from such analysis.

It can also be useful if two or more groups of managers carry out an appraisal independently. Differences of perception can then surface and be discussed, and where agreement is reached some confidence can be placed on the judgements.

It is often useful to carry out several industry/market analyses. The first would be for the industry as a whole; subsequent analyses would focus on particular segments, and a third round might consider the industry at some defined point in the future in order to introduce a dynamic element into what so far had been an exercise in analyzing the current situation. The framework can be valuable then in helping to define strategic segment boundaries, in revealing insights about the key forces in the competitive environment and in revealing which forces can be transformed into advantageous ones by operating proactively upon them, for example by creating switching costs or establishing stronger barriers to entry by building strong brand names.

It can sometimes be useful to rate the strength of each of the five forces to help focus attention on the main competitive factors in each segment, and in order to compare the attractiveness of each segment. A simple points system would rate 1 a weak force and 5 a strong force. Under such a schema an 'attractive' industry would be one scoring 12 points or less. The disadvantage of such a simplistic system is that it ignores the weighting of certain forces that may be necessary. Thus in a patent-dominated industry, or a defence industry, barriers to entry or supplier power respectively would merit above-average weighting. However, this could be allowed for in such a system.

Managers frequently ask 'When I have done a five-force analysis, so what? How can I use it to help me develop my strategy?' The following illustration demonstrates how even the smallest operator can influence the industry structure he/she faces.

Consider the situation where a research scientist is made redundant in mid-career and decides to set up his/her own scientific consultancy company. He/she will need both to assess his/her own core competences, and to conduct a five-force analysis to provide a basis for developing a strategy.

Let us assume that the self-analysis of core competences reveals an energetic, self-starting, personable individual who is an expert in polymerization, with a PhD and twenty years' experience in an ICI

R&D organization. The first attempt at a five-force analysis may be rather depressing, in that it may suggest a market for scientific consultancy services as having high rivalry, low barriers to entry, high threat of substitutes and immense power in the hands of the buyer exemplified in their ability to bargain strongly on fees in the knowledge that the consultant needs the work. When the would-be consultant reaches this point he/she needs to redefine the market so that it relates more closely to his/her core competences. Thus the market for an experienced polymerization scientific consultant is narrower but also more attractive. If the consultant's skills are indeed special the power of the buyer declines, as the consultant is able to demonstrate how he/she can provide the buyer with added value that the buyer cannot get easily elsewhere. Threat of new entrants and of substitutes becomes less as the identified special skills of the consultant erect barriers to entry. Rivalry also becomes less as it becomes clear that he/she has a differentiated service to offer, and the only real rivals are competitors with similar specialist skills.

This five-force situation looks more attractive. The would-be consultant now needs to make it more attractive still by strengthening his/her position further. By a strong marketing effort through writing articles in the trade press, and by personally becoming very visible at trade shows the consultant increases the PUV he/she is able to offer, and thus weakens buyer power, as clients vie for his/her time. The consultant is able to improve the five-force position even further by establishing switching costs in his/her clients. This is done does by personal marketing, by communicating proprietary ideas that the consultant personally needs to help implement, and by building special insight into and knowledge of the company, not possessed by rivals.

In this way, by working on some of the key parameters of the five-force schema, the consultant can carve out a defensible niche position in a market that relates closely to his/her special core competences.

4.7   Competitor analysis

The market environment is obviously key to the identification of opportunities and constraints facing the firm. However, for accurate competitive positioning, a more detailed and specific analysis of the 'rivalry' category of the five-force analysis needs to be carried out by means of an accurate profile of each of the firm's major competitors.

A key part of the environment is composed of the competitors. It is important to understand your competitors well:

1. To try to predict their future strategies.
2. To assess accurately their probable reactions to your strategic moves.
3. To estimate their ability to match you in the quest for sustainable competitive advantage.

Competitor analysis is more important in some industry structures than in others. In terms of five-force analysis the stronger the 'rivalry' force is the more important it is to understand your rivals, since only then can you combat them successfully. In very fragmented industries like hairdressing, for example, competitor analysis may not be crucial to success. Firms are typically small, the product or service may well be undifferentiated, and the key to success not a distinctive competitive strategy, but the provision of a valued service at an acceptable price to a number of locally semi-captive clients. Or the product may be a commodity such as concrete, and price at the required quality the only thing that matters in the buying transaction.

In a concentrated industry, however, competitor analysis is important, since the competitive battle is essentially between a small number of relatively large companies, normally with differentiated products, and often with strong brand names. In such cases, relative market share becomes crucially important, in order to be able to keep down costs by taking advantage of the experience curve, of scale economies and of scope economies as described in Chapters 2 and 3 above.

4.8   Strategic groups

In such circumstances there may be what is often described as a clear strategic group of companies in competition. This situation will lead members of such a group to need to understand the essential strengths and weaknesses of the other members of their group, if they are to succeed competitively.

Strategic groups have been defined in a number of different ways.

However, perhaps the most useful definition is that of groups of companies who are aware of each other as competitors in a particular market, and who are collectively separated from other such groups by mobility barriers. Such barriers vary widely in nature from group to group, and different companies within a group may relate to them to varying degrees. These barriers are the structural characteristics of a market that prevent or at least inhibit one strategic group from merging into another. Mobility barriers may include scale economies, proprietary technology, possession of government licences, control over distribution, marketing power and so forth. Different mobility barriers will be dominant for different strategic groups. The essential importance of the strategic group concept is that it is towards the other members or perhaps potential members of the group that competitor analysis needs to be directed. Rolls-Royce, for example, will not spend its time most valuably by carrying out competitor analysis of Skoda, which is in a quite different group, but it would do well to understand Mercedes Benz's capabilities in some detail.

4.9   The nature of competitor analysis

Competitor analysis is concerned with five basic attributes of the competitor:

1. Its comparative market strength in relation to the key competences required in the industry.
2. Its resources and core competences.
3. Its current and possible future strategy.
4. Its culture, and hence the assumptions it makes about itself and the industry.
5. Its objectives and goals both at corporate and at business unit level.

Comparative market strength

This can be assessed by using the Producer Matrix described in Chapter 3. In order to complete this matrix it is necessary to identify the essential elements of Perceived Use Value (PUV) on the Customer Matrix (see Chapter 2), and from this derive the key competences needed to be able to provide these elements of PUV in the product offering (see Chapter 3).

The next step is to identify the company's main competitors, and collect sufficient data and opinions in relation to them to make a comparative assessment of each of them and of the company itself.

The competences are then assessed for relative importance and given a weighting accordingly. (See Figures 3.2 and 3.3 above.)

It is common to include market share as an internal criterion along with the more direct factors. This is because a strong market share, although more a result than a cause of strength, may help the company achieve low costs through the experience curve and scale economies in particular.

Competitor analysis needs to be carried out on a segment-by-segment basis. In this way the specific key competences necessary to achieve competitive advantage in each segment are compared firm by firm. Where the key competence profiles for related segments are similar this allows firms to enter adjoining segments without substantially needing to build new competences; that is, it reflects a broadly based set of core competences.

This form of comparative competitor analysis is inevitably imprecise, as it is generally based on judgements rather than on precise data. However, the Producer Matrix and its back-up charts provide a valuable, graphic way of comparing all the members of a strategic group in terms of the key competences relevant to producing what the market requires. Its precision can be improved in direct proportion to the firm's efforts and abilities to collect accurate data on the competitor.

Resources and core competences

The resources and core competences of the competitor need to be determined by the same method as that used for the analyst company, as set out in the previous chapter. The only major difference is the problem that to gather the necessary data from a competitor is inevitably far more difficult than for one's own firm. However, the process needs to be done and is part of the same exercise as that described above in compiling a file on the competitors. The overall core competence assessment can be illustrated on the same type of graph as that used for internal core and key competence analysis for both operations and systems (see Figures 3.2 and 3.3).

Current strategy

The current strategy of competitors is discernible partly from what the company has to say, but more importantly from what it does. To assess either factor, a positive effort will need to be made at competitor data collection, in excess of the information that will easily come the company's way through a conscientious reading of the press. Effective competitor analysis requires the creation of a file on each competitor, and its active maintenance in up-to-date condition, by an enthusiastic executive who can act as 'champion' for the specific task. In the absence of such conditions, the file is likely to become outdated after a few months.

The company's intended, or at least declared, strategy can usually be discovered from the chairman's message to shareholders in annual reports, and by interviews in the press given by competitor senior personnel. The competitor's realized strategy is, however, the more important, and this can only be discovered by tracking the competitor's actions over a period of time, and scanning it for consistency of purpose. Such direct observation can be supplemented by deliberately seeking out comment from suppliers who deal with both the analyst company and the competition, by interviewing buyers, by recruiting and debriefing executives from competitor companies, and by talking to journalists and other industry analysts. It is particularly important to gain early information of a competitor's possible change of strategy, and this may be signalled in a number of ways: by comment, by an unusual acquisition, by announced personnel changes at the top and so forth.

The competitor's culture

This is normally an important factor in setting limits to the actions the competitor is likely to take in a market. An understanding of that culture will reveal the way the company operates, and the constraints within which it often subconsciously operates. A company's culture embodies the core values that executives in the company take for granted. An understanding of this can be very valuable to a competitor. A popular method for graphically illustrating this culture is to draw up a culture web of the company (see Johnson and Scholes 1993), which, if constructed with insight, will often reveal weaknesses and limitations in the competitor's essential method of operation of value to the analyst. Whilst collecting data

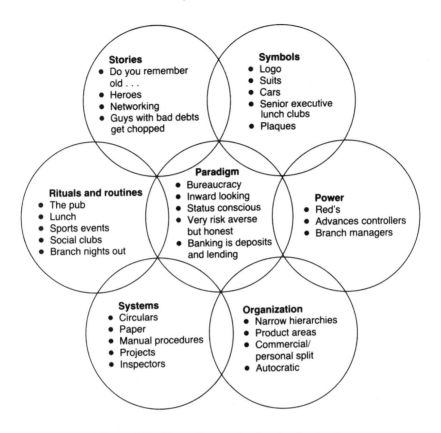

Figure 4.2 The culture web of a clearing bank

for culture web construction, the analyst will also gain insights into the assumptions the competitor habitually makes about itself and its industry. Figure 4.2 illustrates the traditional culture web of a clearing bank.

Objectives

The objectives of the competitors are the fifth factor to be assessed in a competitor analysis exercise. A company concerned to achieve short-term financial objectives, for example, is likely to react quite differently from one with longer-term market share objectives willing to take perhaps a ten-year view to establish its position in the market.

If the competitor is a subsidiary of a major corporation, it is also necessary to understand the basic objectives of the parent. A company owned by the Hanson Group, for example, is likely to be far more constrained in terms of research and development expenditure, or in adopting a new initiative with a long gestation time, than would a company that is part of the Shell Group, accustomed as it is to the high risks associated with oil exploration. The level of autonomy the competitor possesses, in seeking to achieve its objectives, is also relevant to the competitor assessment exercise.

4.10   Summary

Market environment analysis may be carried out by means of the five-force model, which assesses the relative strengths of industry rivalry, the power of buyers and suppliers and the threat of entry by new competitors marketing similar products or substitute products. This schema can lead to valuable insights into the relative strength of the underlying forces operating in the industry.

A competitor analysis exercise will give a more accurate picture of the precise strength of the firm's major rivals. It is concerned to discover a number of basic factors about competitor companies, in order to understand them better, when facing them in the market-place. The most important of these factors are: the competitor's market strength, in respect of the key required competences, its current and likely future strategy, its culture and its fundamental objectives.

Equipped with competitor information able to determine these factors, the analyst will be in a strong position to address such key questions in competitor analysis as the following:

1. Is the competitor satisfied with its current market position, or is it likely to become aggressive in the near future?
2. Where is the competitor most vulnerable?
3. Is it likely to change strategy in the near future? If so, how?
4. What action by us is likely to provoke the greatest/least retaliation by the competitors?
5. In what areas might it be possible to cooperate with the competitors?

6. How might we shift the basis of competition in the market towards qualities in which we have excellence?

It is based on answers to questions such as these that new ideas for achieving competitive advantage may be developed.

5

The future

Although a thorough analysis of the current competitive situation is helpful in determining competitive strategy, having an accurate view of how the future environment might unfold can provide even more valuable insights, which can help the firm achieve an additional competitive edge. However, as Michael Naylor of General Motors once said: 'Strategic Planning faces one big problem. There are no facts about the future, only opinions.' If the world were logical and predictable, forecasting the future could rely on statistical techniques, extrapolating trends discernible from the past. However, research has shown that econometric models are typically unreliable for more than two quarters into the future, and judgemental forecasts are as good or even better. Economic forecasting in fact has much in common with long-range weather forecasting. The number and variability of the strength of the forces impacting on the economy are such that the probability of accurate prediction must generally be very low.

This view is borne out by a consideration of some of the major largely unforecast world events of recent years, notably, the dissolution of the Soviet Union, the reunification of Germany, the movement of the developed nations from largely social welfare economies to market-led ideologies, the democratization of Latin America, but the crushing of the democracy movement in China, and until recently the rapid acceleration of EC economic integration.

But this record is counterbalanced to some extent by the list of correctly forecast major world trends, notably the continuing rise of Far East economic power, the dramatic improvements in communications due largely to micro-chip technology, the ever-increasing level of automation in a growing number of industries, and the continued globalization of consumer tastes and markets. Some useful forecasting may therefore probably be worthwhile so long as it is not single-point forecasting, and does not attempt to be too precise. Trends, it would seem, are easier to forecast than events. Changes in the Customer and Producer Matrices are likely to be more predictable over the short term e.g. 1–2 years, based on the current knowledge of customers and producers. However, in order to assess changes in the medium- to longer-term future, say 2–10 years ahead, other approaches are required like scenario building, and assessing the political, economic, social and technological trends in the firm's environment. In this chapter, we put forward an integrated set of techniques, which can be used to probe the future industry environment. We begin by examining how the two basic matrices introduced in previous chapters, the Customer Matrix and the Producer Matrix, may change. Then the broader environmental context is explored using two well-established techniques, PEST (Political, Economic, Social and Technological) analysis and scenario building.

5.1   Changes in the Customer Matrix

To summarize: the two axes of the Customer Matrix are Perceived Price and Perceived Use Value. Once the relative positions of competitors' product offerings have been established (see Figure 5.1) a number of questions should be addressed:

- Is demand in this segment expanding or contracting?
- In which direction are the existing individual products likely to move?
- Will the dimensions of PUV change, either through a change in the relative importance of the PUV dimensions, or through the introduction of new ones? Remember that a shift in the dimensions of PUV will most probably alter the relative positions of competitors on the Customer Matrix.
- Will the elements of Perceived Price alter, for example away from concern with purchase price towards the long-term cost of ownership? Again shifts in the elements of Perceived Price are likely to affect the relative positions of competitors on the matrix.

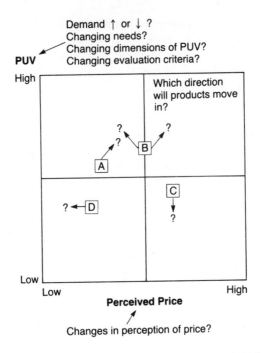

Figure 5.1   The Customer Matrix: looking ahead

5.2   Changes in the Producer Matrix

A similar set of questions can be addressed in relation to the Producer Matrix (see Figure 5.2). The axes of this matrix are Effectiveness and Unit Costs, and they reflect the strength of the core competences of the firm in relation to those of its competitors. An important issue concerning the Producer Matrix, and hence the Customer Matrix also, is the likelihood of new competitors entering the market. A new competitor can enter and gain advantage either through being able to undercut the existing players on unit costs, or through the possession of superior key competences, or both at the same time. In order to assess the likelihood of entry, the two axes of the Producer Matrix need to be analyzed into their constituent parts.

The ability of firms to move on the Producer Matrix, and the ease with which new firms can enter the industry are determined by the firm's ability to control the activity cost drivers, and to develop the relevant key competences. New competitors are more likely to enter

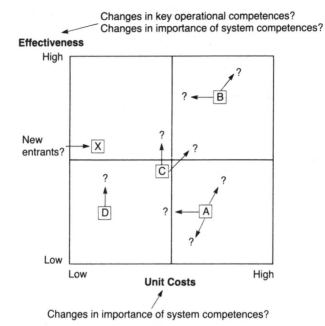

Figure 5.2 The Producer Matrix: looking ahead

from existing industries that have similar operational and systems competences: for example, the Taiwanese high-technology sports goods company Kunnan has recently entered the personal computer market under the Arche brand name, basing its competitive claims on its systems competence in procurement, its marketing skills and its lean high-technology manufacturing processes, including excellent quality assurance.

The relative cost positions of firms in the industry are determined by the factors underlying costs, many of which may stem from the state of the macro-economic environment, and from the existing state of the dominant technology in the industry. In order to develop a fuller picture of the evolution of the Customer and Producer Matrices, therefore, the wider environmental context must be considered.

Using existing information on competitors, and current understanding about customers and their needs, it should be possible to develop a view about how firms will move on the Customer and Producer Matrices in the near future (indicated by arrows in Figures

5.1 and 5.2). These probable shifts will affect the competitive balance in the market, leading to changes in relative market shares.

However, in order to gain insights into the medium- to longer-term development of the industry, say three to ten years ahead, it is necessary to explore the broader environmental context of the industry. This can be done firstly by carrying out a PEST analysis, and then by developing a number of alternative scenarios of possible futures for the industry.

5.3   PEST analysis

A PEST checklist (see Figure 5.3) helps the analyst to carry out this process. Perhaps trends can more easily be predicted than events, and the PEST checklist, as shown in Figure 5.3, provides a useful list of factors to consider in trying to forecast the changing nature of the forces likely to have an impact on the industry over the next few years. PEST analysis can be combined with five-force analysis to develop a view of the future structure of an industry. It is also a useful start for planning the development of a number of possible scenarios.

5.4   Scenarios

In many forcasting situations scenario planning is a useful technique to adopt. Scenario planning is most appropriate for industries that have a high level of capital intensity, and a relatively long lead time for product development. Industries that involve a high level of risk also benefit from the scenario approach. Only in such industries is it necessary to take a fairly long-term look into the future. If the lead time for product development is short, it is possible to react to events as they appear, and a 'trading' type of mentality may be more appropriate than a crystal-gazing one. If the industry is not capital-intensive an incremental approach can be taken to development, the essence of which is to maintain flexibility. In these circumstances, therefore, time spent on scenario planning may not be well used. Both characteristics should be present in an industry to at least a moderate degree before scenario planning becomes a necessary strategic tool. Thus service sectors like management consultancy, public relations, advertising or market trading may

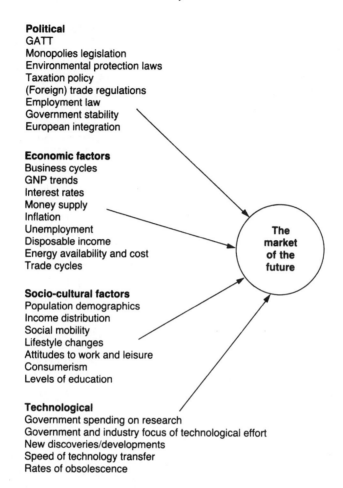

Political
GATT
Monopolies legislation
Environmental protection laws
Taxation policy
(Foreign) trade regulations
Employment law
Government stability
European integration

Economic factors
Business cycles
GNP trends
Interest rates
Money supply
Inflation
Unemployment
Disposable income
Energy availability and cost
Trade cycles

Socio-cultural factors
Population demographics
Income distribution
Social mobility
Lifestyle changes
Attitudes to work and leisure
Consumerism
Levels of education

Technological
Government spending on research
Government and industry focus of technological effort
New discoveries/developments
Speed of technology transfer
Rates of obsolescence

The market of the future

Figure 5.3   The PEST factors

have little need for scenario planning. For the oil, steel or engineering industries, however, the technique is becoming increasingly vital, if the chances of major investment mistakes are to be minimized.

Generally, where the risks are high, the development of more than one scenario provides some hedge against error, although inevitably such a hedge can be only a limited one. You can still get it badly wrong even with scenario planning.

A scenario is a self-contained envelope of consistent possibilities which describes the future. A scenario contains events that the strategist cannot control. If they can be controlled they represent strategic choices.

There are two main types of scenario, the quantitative and the qualitative. The quantitative method of scenario building is based on mathematical (econometric) forecasting, using computer models and a number of simulations using different values of the parameters. Probability estimates are attached to each scenario. The relationships between the variables are assessed, and the likely impact on one variable of a change in the value of another. Attempts are made to structure and formalize what must initially be judgemental forecasting of the key parameters. Using such quantitative methods, a large number of alternative scenarios can easily be generated on a computer. The quantitative method, however, suffers from the weakness that the seeming precision of the models tends to make the scenario planner forget that all models are built on past relationships, which may well not be future relationships. Furthermore the model is only as good as the initial parameters allow, and these are necessarily judgemental, and thus subject to an indeterminate band of error.

The qualitative approach is most commonly traced back to the 1950s and the work of Herman Kahn. Believers in qualitative methods tend to distrust the value of quantification, considering that well-judged underlying assumptions are much more important than sophisticated methodologies. They contend that the future carries an infinite number of variables and values, and therefore any attempt to select a few and compute their implications is quite pointless. They put their faith instead in intuition, and the value of an integrative and holistic approach. They are conscious that the possibility of predicting the future in even a rough-and-ready way is very remote, and therefore believe that the best way forward is to make intuitive guesses structured around known trends, plus selected possible themes for consistent views of the future.

Scenario planning serves three major purposes:

1. It looks into the future and thus attempts to anticipate events, and to understand risk.

2. It provides the ideas for entrepreneurial activity, by identifying new possibly unthought-of strategic options.

3. It helps managers to break out of their established mental constraints and become aware of possible futures other than those which merely represent a measured extrapolation of the present.

It enables managers to gain a better understanding of the forces driving business systems to develop a feel for the direction of those forces, to understand the logical implications of events already in the pipeline, to appreciate the interdependencies in the system and to become able to rule out the impossible, whilst accepting the inevitable. It is, for example, probably impossible for the UK economy to grow at 10 per cent a year like the Chinese economy seems to be doing, and it is probably inevitable that the United Kingdom will face the need to support an ageing population over the next quarter century.

5.5 A proposed scenario-planning method

The following seven-step methodology for scenario planning is based on the qualitative approach. It is built around the requirement to generate three possible scenarios for the future, each of which represents an internally consistent view of the world often usefully expressed in the form of a theme, such as the 'Green' revolution. It uses two central concepts for identifying scenarios, and for relating them to the company concerned, namely 'key determinants' and 'principal impact factors'.

Key determinants are the major events or trends predicted to happen in the future in relation to the economic world. The events following from the GATT negotiations will be key determinants, for example, as would be a recession in continental Europe. More specifically a downward or upward trend in interest rates would be key determinants.

Principal impact factors, however, reflect the likely impact of the key determinants on the enterprise. A key determinant of an interest rate rise would have a principal impact factor effect of an increase in the cost of capital, probably coupled with fall in demand, and a decline in investment.

Key determinants and principal impact factors do not necessarily, or even usually, have a one-to-one relationship. One key determinant may have an impact on a company in several ways, and contrastingly one impact factor may change as a result of a number of key determinants. Thus a rise in interest rates will have an impact on a company by raising the cost of borrowing, by reducing investment and lowering demand; that is, three impact factors from one key determinant. The reverse may also apply and three or more key determinants may affect one impact factor. Thus sharp economic growth, lowered taxes and a change of tastes in the market may as key determinants all affect the impact factor level of demand.

Step 1: scan the environment

The first step in scenario planning is to develop a profile of the current environment. This would include the following components:

1. A five-force environmental analysis.
2. A short list of relevant economic 'inevitable' and 'impossible' factors, to provide boundaries to the crystal gazing.
3. The identification of key trends currently discernible from world events, derived from a PEST analysis.

It is often useful to employ a panel of experts to help in the completion of this step, since it sets the scene for the scenario development, and is therefore important to get right. Delphi techniques may be useful here. Thus the experts give their uninfluenced opinions. They are then informed of the opinions of the other experts, and asked to revise their opinions in the light of this new information. By such a method some of the problems of 'groupthink' often encountered in expert panels are avoided; that is, all the participants' thinking is in accord with the dominant personality or leader figure.

Step 2: conduct an internal analysis

Although scenario planning is concerned with the external world, and not specifically with the company, it is nevertheless important, before developing the scenarios, to prepare a summary profile of the company. The reason for this is to enable the scenario planner to choose the most relevant and appropriate key determinants, and principal impact factors, as they should be factors with a potentially large effect on the company. For example, if the company has no borrowings, an interest rate rise and consequent increase in the cost of borrowing might not be chosen respectively as key determinants and principal impact factors. If the interest rate rise is steep, however, for such a company, the impact factor might be a decline in the level of demand resulting from it. The company profile should include the following:

1. An activity cost analysis of the firm and its linkages both 'upstream' and 'downstream' to suppliers and retailers respectively.
2. Identification of the company's core competences.
3. Data on the company's financial, marketing, production, technology and personnel resources.
4. Mission statement and objectives.
5. Key strategies.
6. Culture and leadership style.
7. Competitive position within its major markets, and a list and assessments of its key competitors. These could be in the form of Customer and Producer Matrices for its major markets.

Step 3: develop three scenarios

Three scenarios should be developed, of which one should be a 'no surprises' scenario, developing the implications of current economic trends, adjusted to take note of known current and future 'inevitable' events. The other two scenarios should depict possible alternative views of the future. The scenarios are described in terms of their key determinants (see Figure 5.4). For example, a possible scenario-planning exercise for the private health-care market in the United Kingdom in the medium-term future might go as in the following subsections.

No surprises	Government underfunding	Private health care becomes very expensive
Level of government NHS funding as at present	Government underfunds NHS	Government reforms make NHS very effective
Pressure on resources due to ageing population	Ageing population	Ageing population
Growth of fitter lifestyles	Increase in stress diseases	Improved lifestyles
Technology change reduces invasive surgery	Slowing of technological change	Fast technological growth
Increasing sophistication of consumer	Scramble for health care reduces consumer power	Consumer becomes very selective

Figure 5.4 Key determinants

Scenario 1: no surprises

The government would continue to fund the health area as at present. The growth of demand in the private sector would be slow, due to static economic conditions, and hence limited real income growth. The ageing population, however, would lead to increasing pressure on resources, although this would be mitigated to some extent by increased fitness lifestyles incrementally reducing some key killer diseases like heart disease. Technology advances would continue to make surgical invasion less traumatic, but at considerable cost in new capital equipment. Finally the consumer would continue to become more sophisticated in the choice of health-care provision.

Scenario 2: the government underfunds health

This would probably lead to fast growth in the private sector to compensate for the government's underprovision. The healthy lifestyle movement shows a reversal, and increasingly stressful living leads to an increase in stress-related diseases. The ageing population continues to increase demand for health provision. Technology development in the sector slows down. Consumer demand becomes less sophisticated as there is a scramble for health-care services.

Scenario 3: the private health-care market becomes very expensive

The economy declines and incomes to buy health insurance become insufficient for the average target family. The government, through increased resource provision, generous payments to budget-holding GPs and active development of NHS trust hospitals, causes a steep decline in the private medical insurance market. Fitness lifestyles improve the health of the nation despite the ageing population. Fast advances in technology continue. Finally the decline in demand makes the consumer extremely selective in his/her private health-care investment.

For each scenario the impact factors of the key determinants identified above should be listed, and their force assessed.

In order to arrive at the most appropriate scenario themes, it may be necessary to identify the key determinants first, before deciding upon a theme. An iterative process may be necessary, between theme selection and key determinant identification, before internally consistent scenarios can be agreed upon.

It is important not to select three scenarios characterized as (1) optimistic, (2) medium and (3) pessimistic scenarios for the following reasons. Such titles do little more than place a band of error around the medium scenario, which is not the aim of the exercise. Secondly a scenario depicts a set of world events. It cannot be classified as optimistic or otherwise until the firm's strategy has been determined. It cannot be said, for example, whether a 'Europeanization' scenario, or a 'Green lifestyles' one is optimistic or pessimistic. This depends upon how effectively the firm responds to the unfolding events.

Whilst it is important not to select simplistic optimistic, medium and pessimistic scenarios, however, it is probably useful to select scenarios that do represent opposite ends of the spectrum in relation to such key impact factors as demand levels. If only strongly growing demand is considered there will be no contingency plans for potentially more difficult conditions.

Step 4: apply principal impact factors

The next stage in the process is to apply the impact factors to each of the scenarios, as shown in Figure 5.5. The principal areas of concern in the private health-care sector are judged to be the following:

A. The level of costs.
B. The level and nature of competition.
C. The level of prices.

1. Extension of current trends.
2. Government underfunds health.
3. Private health care becomes too expensive.

Principal impact factors	1	2	3
A. Costs	Slow rise	Slow rise	Fast rise
B. Level and nature of competition	Slowly increasing	Decreases short term	Tougher
C. Market prices	Downward pressure	Rise	Downward pressure of demand
D. Level of day care	Increasing	Up	Up
E. Opportunities for expansion	Limited	Good	Poor
F. Demand	Static	Rise	Fall

Figure 5.5 Themes for scenarios

D. The extent of the growth of day care.

E. The opportunities for expansion.

F. The strength of demand.

The movement of these impact factors is then judged in relation to each scenario, given the forecast nature of the key determinants. For example, scenario 3 predicts a situation in which private health care prices itself out of the market; this affects competitors by making competition tougher as the same number of companies fight for a share of a smaller market.

Step 5: the scenario matrix

The next step is to place all the evaluated impact factors on a scenario matrix, as shown in Figure 5.6. The two axes of the matrix are 'probability of occurrence' on the vertical axis, and 'strategic importance of factor' on the horizontal axis. Thus impact factor A applied to scenario 1 would be coded as A1 (a slow rise in costs) and must be assessed for its strategic importance and its probability of occurrence. If both are rated as high, the factor is placed in the top right-hand quadrant of the matrix. Quadrant 1 is that from which the ultimate chosen most likely scenario will be selected. The dotted lines show the quadrant to be larger than a quarter of the whole

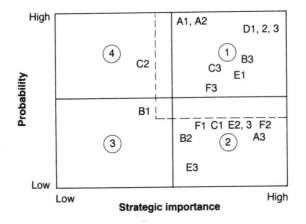

Figure 5.6 The Scenario Matrix: the private health care market

matrix, since even a 40 per cent level of probability and strategic impact justifies inclusion in the chosen scenario.

When all factors have been assessed for impact and probability for all three scenarios, they may well spread across all four quadrants.

Step 6: select the most likely scenario

In quadrant 1 and immediately adjacent to it are the factors rated as applying to the most probable scenario, and with the greatest assessed level of strategic importance. The factors in this quadrant will almost certainly be a combination of the factors from two or more initial scenarios. These factors have been rated as both most probable and also most strategically important. In the example of the private health-care market the chosen scenario is characterized at impact factor level as one in which the following occur:

1. Costs rise inexorably (A1, A2).
2. Competition becomes tougher (B3).
3. Prices face downward pressure, largely because of weakening demand, and increasing competitor provision (C3).
4. Day care increases, exacerbating the downward pressure on prices (D1, 2, 3).
5. Opportunities for expansion are limited (E1).
6. Demand falls (F3).

The above impact factors from the chosen scenario, after some screening and adjustment for consistency, form the basis of the scenario on which strategy is to be based.

Step 7: prepare contingency plans

Any factors in quadrant 4 would be likely to happen but are judged to be strategically unimportant. They should therefore be accepted as congruent with the chosen scenario, but not highlighted as important factors in the strategic process. Factors in quadrant 3 would also be unimportant strategically, but they are also unlikely to occur. They should therefore be discounted.

The factors in quadrant 2, however, should not be discounted. They are not regarded as likely to come about, but if by chance they do (and scenarios can be by their very nature no more than best guesses) then their strategic importance is great. Contingency plans should therefore be prepared that are able to cope with these factors if they do come about. In the illustration contingency plans should be prepared for factors A3, B2, C1, E2, E3, F1 and F2. This means plans should be prepared for the contingencies that costs rise faster than expected, competition becomes far tougher (downward pressure on prices has already been allowed for in C3); opportunities for expansion should be responded to sensitively even if they are unexpected, and the firm should not be caught napping if demand expands dramatically contrary to expectations.

This is the great strength of the scenario-planning process. It enables strategy to be changed to activate already prepared contingency plans, in the event that a scenario different from the chosen one starts to develop. It cannot be guaranteed that the deviation from the selected scenario will necessarily be in the direction of the contingency plans, but at least the preparation of such plans establishes the mind-set that accepts strategic change in response to unexpected outcomes as a normal event.

5.6 Summary

The major benefits of scenario planning are then the following:

1. It challenges the conventional wisdom.
2. It demonstrates the possible impact of a lot of 'what if?' questions.
3. It enables contingency plans to be developed for strategically important but low-probability events.
4. It helps to clarify the interrelationships between key impact factors that affect the company.
5. Finally it establishes the mind-set that accepts uncertainty, and finds it less of a threat and more of an opportunity to profit at the expense of a less far-sighted competitor.

Understanding the forces likely to create the future is crucially important to a competitive strategist. Consideration of the Consumer and Producer Matrices, and how they will change, enables the strategist to look towards the future in a structured way. The PEST checklist is also useful in this process and can help with scenario development. Scenario planning goes some limited way towards coping with the problem that exists because the future cannot be known and strategies have to be selected in conditions of uncertainty. By developing three different scenarios around consistent themes, and analyzing them by key determinants and principal impact factors, strategists are able to construct a more robust strategy than by the use of single-point forecasting. They are also, through consideration of alternative scenarios, able to develop contingency plans to deal with some unexpected eventualities.

6

Strategic choice

Having selected the strategic direction it is intending to pursue on the Customer Matrix at an overall firm level, the company strategist must now go to the next decision level in order to select the markets, products and methods to be adopted in order to achieve the sought-after and elusive sustainable competitive advantage. This involves the consideration of risk, and the evaluation of specific moves in the light of this.

The Customer Matrix at a general level can be used to represent the overall company strategic stance (e.g. Rolls-Royce, very up-market and expensive; Skoda, rather down-market and budget-priced). However, to be usable for specific strategy formulation, the matrix needs to be formulated for a particular product/market situation. It represents the firm's position relative to its competitors in relation to PUV and Perceived Price. Any movement on it refers to the same product in the same market. The Producer Matrix, however, is concerned with effectiveness and cost efficiency competences as they apply to a particular product group and market, but may well reflect the firm's overall competences in a variety of areas to a greater degree than the Customer Matrix can.

6.1 Combinations of Customer and Producer Matrices

There are potentially a large number of combinations of positions on the Customer and Producer Matrices. In Figure 6.1 we have set out

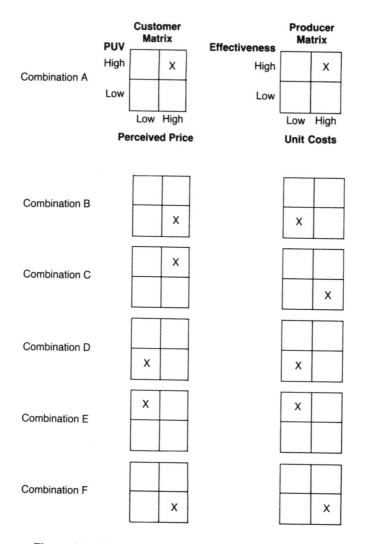

Figure 6.1 Combinations of Customer and Producer Matrices

six of the more likely combinations. We shall briefly examine each of these to explore what strategic response might be appropriate to them. Note, however, that we are not advocating a crude and simplistic set of prescriptions; we are merely pointing out some potentially viable options that might be explored.

Combination A

Here the firm is currently premium pricing on the basis of offering higher than average PUV. On the Producer Matrix we can see that the firm, perhaps not surprisingly, compares favourably with its competitors with regard to effectiveness. However, the firm is relatively inefficient. This can often be the result of the ability to command premium prices.

This can have three effects: firstly, the price premiums tend to allow the firm to operate at less than optimal levels of cost efficiency; secondly, beliefs in a strong brand image and/or quality reputation can encourage the management to think that cost reduction is not a pressing priority; and thirdly, an effect of premium prices might be that relative market shares are smaller, reducing the firm's ability to benefit from any cost advantages that might accrue from scale or experience effects.

A key issue here is the sustainability of the price premium. If this is based on operational competences, such as leading edge technology development, then the issue is how reproducible this competence is. If a competitor could acquire this competence then the firm might find itself under threat. If the operational competence is, say, a strong brand image, then the premium price positioning may be more defensible, as long as the brand's image can be sustained.

If the advantage is derived from more generic systems competences, such as value assurance processes, then the likelihood of a competitor matching or surpassing the firm may be less, as these competences are built into the fabric of the firm and are inherently difficult to imitate.

Of course once a competitor offers equivalent PUV, the price premium is likely to be competed away. The resulting positioning for the firm would be: average price, above-average or average PUV, depending on how many competitors could imitate the higher levels of PUV, combined with an above-average cost position. Relative profitability would then be poor. However, it might be possible for the firm to shift perceptions of price, so that it achieves a move west on the matrix without actually cutting list prices; for example, Mercedes attempts to shift price perceptions away from initial purchase price to overall costs of ownership, including regard to resale value.

So, prescriptions for a firm in this position might be the following:

- Defend the bases of differentiation such as the brand or the ability to innovate.

- Pay greater attention to cost reduction, factor costs or improved coordination and control in order to improve relative position on the horizontal axis of the Producer Matrix.

Combination B

Low relative PUV and above-average pricing in this example will lead to decreasing market share in all circumstances other than a severe supply constraint, such as a monopoly supplier. Such a position can be avoided by cutting price, as the firm has the low cost position to permit this. However, if the effectiveness competences on the Producer Matrix cannot be improved, the firm will be restricted to a down-market positioning.

Unfortunately if the competitors leverage their relatively stronger effectiveness competences into the offering of higher and higher levels of PUV, this firm may find itself having to discount prices heavily, in order to persuade customers to accept the inferior package of PUV being offered to them.

One option may be to explore other markets, where the firm's products would not be seen to have relatively low levels of PUV, for example selling the Rover Montego in Russia. But then the firm would be facing another Producer and Customer Matrix, and the relative cost position on the Producer Matrix might present a problem, for instance the factor costs of indigenous Russian car producers might be much lower. Alternatively, the firm may be able to improve its effectiveness competences through alliances.

Combination C

In this example, the firm has successfully achieved the position of a premium-priced differentiator; however, it has below-average effectiveness and efficiency. This situation can arise when past levels of investment in, say, product development, R&D or brand image building have been strong, but have not been sustained into the present. The firm has been, in effect, resting on its laurels. The higher relative cost levels cannot be explained away by higher current expenditures on developing the firm's effectiveness. Higher relative costs resulting from poor cost disciplines would mean that profit margins would be no better than average. This situation can also arise where a firm is good at innovation (a system competence) but it is unable to transfer these developments into saleable products. The firm's value enhancement and value assurance competences would probably be inferior to those of competitors. As with the EMI Scanner, the inventing company EMI scored highly on innovation, but was unable to capitalize on this in profit terms, due to its deficiencies in marketing and other effectiveness competences.

The fact that competitor firms have higher effectiveness competences would suggest that it is only a matter of time before these competences will move competitors north on the Customer Matrix. The prognosis for this firm is not good. The urgent need to improve both effectiveness and efficiency with only average levels of profitability presents a major problem.

Interestingly, the managers' perception of the firm's situation may be quite different from that revealed by this analysis. If, as is often the case, managers are not sufficiently well informed about their position on the Producer Matrix, because the required information on competitors is not routinely collected, they might see their firm as being in a very strong position. They would make this judgement from their ability currently to sell at premium prices. Therefore in the absence of a sense of crisis, the tendency would be to maintain the status quo in an atmosphere of complacency.

If, however, the management are aware of the firm's predicament, then it is probably necessary in the short term for them to prioritize either improving effectiveness or cost efficiency, that is, trying to move either north or west on the Producer Matrix, rather than attempting to do both things simultaneously. Unless there is focus on either effectiveness or cost efficiency the danger is that efforts will be dissipated over too broad a set of actions. Typically, cutting costs is easier to achieve as a short-term strategy than building operational competences. A major focus on cost reduction will signal that radical change is necessary, and this may help to build a momentum for the introduction of further changes designed to improve effectiveness.

An alternative approach may be to subcontract some activities to more efficient suppliers, thus reducing the amount of work done in-house, and enabling the firm to concentrate on improving effectiveness.

Combination D

The firm in this example is offering low PUV at a low price. It has a high level of efficiency combined with low effectiveness. As in combination B there is a danger that, unless effectiveness can be improved, the firm will find itself having to offer larger price discounts as competitors' products move further north in the matrix.

This situation is often reached by new low-cost entrants to established markets, such as Korean (Hyundai) and Malaysian (Proton) car manufacturers. Using product designs, engines and production systems developed by other car manufacturers, they have been able to penetrate the lower end of the car market in Europe and North America. However, unless they are prepared to develop their effectiveness competences, they may be condemned to operate in the down-market segment of the world car market.

Japanese companies have shown that this entry strategy need not prevent the subsequent development of the required competences to design and build high-quality products, such as cars, hi-fi equipment, cameras and photocopiers. Strategic alliances may be one route to gaining the required operational and systems competences that the firm currently lacks.

Combination E

This combination is the one to aim at. It implies high levels of PUV, and currently unbeatably competitive pricing, based on a strong Producer Matrix position of excellent effectiveness and efficiency competences, able to sustain the Customer Matrix position into the future.

Possible problems might be management complacency, or it might be that demand in this segment may be shrinking. There may be the option to raise price if rivals are unable to match the high PUV. The increased surpluses that should result could be used to outpace rivals with strong investment in both effectiveness and efficiency.

The firm might also explore other product markets where its core competences might confer similar advantages, since a strong Producer Matrix position may well be transferable into an equally strong one in other segments without the need for major changes of emphasis.

Combination F

This combination is the opposite of combination E. It reflects high prices and low PUV, linked with low competences in both cost efficiency and effectiveness. A firm in such a position faces a fight for survival. The key question must be: How difficult is it for the

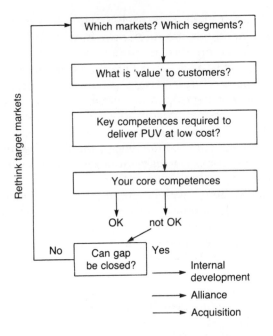

Figure 6.2   Deriving a competitive strategy

firm to move north-west on the Producer Matrix, that is, to increase both its relative effectiveness and efficiency? It may be possible to institute a programme of cost cutting, coupled with the recruitment of some additional expertise to close the gap with competitors.

If the task is too large to bridge by internal development, the solution may be approached through alliances or even merger, acquisition or being taken over. The position reflected by combination F requires drastic measures if it is to be converted into one from which profitable survival may be confidently predicted.

6.2   The risk cube

Figure 6.2 above summarizes the decision processes involved in formulating a competitive strategy. An initial choice of target markets and target segments, followed by an identification of what customers value in these segments, leads to the question of what the firm needs to do well to deliver what the customer wants.

From a consideration of the competences required, the firm will need to assess what competences it actually has, and has been able to demonstrate in the present and recent past. If these competences meet those needed then 'OK'.

If the firm's competences are necessary but not sufficient to achieve competitive advantage in the chosen segments, then the firm needs to set about closing the gap, either by internal action, by forming an alliance or by acquisition.

If this cannot be done successfully, then perhaps competitive advantage is not attainable in the chosen segment, and the firm will need to loop back to reconsider the segment in which it should choose to compete.

As in combination F above, a firm may not be able to achieve competitive advantage in its current product market segment. In which case it will need to consider other options, for example marketing the same product to a different market. This will involve the construction of a different Customer Matrix and perhaps even some adjustment of the Producer Matrix. Similarly a further option may be to market a different product to the same market. This will involve a different Producer Matrix as the relevant competences and costs will be different, and perhaps a lesser adjustment to the Customer Matrix.

For each combination of product offering and market (represented by PUV) distinct Customer and Producer Matrices will need to be developed before the potential competitive strength of the firm in the identified situation can be assessed, and a strategic direction selected. Once product/market options have been listed and placed on their relevant matrices, each needs to be assessed for relative risk.

Options can be analyzed in terms of direction and of method. Both factors involve risk. Thus under the heading of direction we will consider which markets to operate in and which products and services to produce, noting that risk increases the further away both the markets and the products get from those in which we are currently active.

Under the heading of method we will encompass internal development, joint development or alliance, and acquisition; categories are once more in ascending levels of risk. Clearly, it is not rational to adopt a greater level of risk to achieve a desired objective if that same objective is attainable taking less risk. Generally the rational person would not attempt to jump over a ten-foot-wide river to get to the other bank, if there were a convenient bridge to walk over at virtually no risk whatsoever.

The risk cube (see Figure 6.3) illustrates the options open to the strategist, with the ascending arrow going into the back of the cube

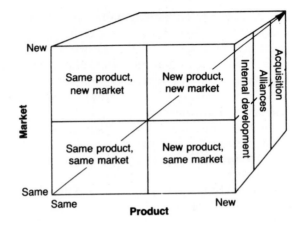

Note: Risk increases with movement away from current activities by:

- Product.
- Market.
- Corporate Activity.

Figure 6.3 The risk cube

representing increasing risk. Thus the lowest-risk option is to continue to sell the same products and services into the same market, and to attempt to grow by internal development. However, such a strategy may not realize acceptable results. The market may be saturated and/or the product obsolescent or at least in decline. In this event, the next options to be considered, in ascending risk terms, are to supply a new product to the present market, or to market the present product to a new market. Only in exceptional circumstances should the excessively high-risk option be considered of marketing an unfamiliar product to an unfamiliar market. This would be the equivalent in risk of a mountain climber jumping from one foothold to another, a recipe for probable ultimate tragedy.

The risk element of these moves is increased if the firm attempts to make any of the above moves by methods other than internal development. Joint development involves operating with a partner with whom one is unfamiliar, and over whom one has very limited control. This increases the level of uncertainty, and hence of risk.

Development by acquisition increases risk even further, since it involves purchasing an unfamiliar company, which is likely to have been marketed in such a way as to maximize the price the seller is able to achieve. On conclusion of the acquisition, therefore, the purchaser will not only need time to establish the real value of the assets purchased, but may be in control of a top management team substantially demotivated or depleted as a result of the ownership transfer. This option is likely to be the highest risk and the most expensive one. If the acquired company operates with unfamiliar products in markets unfamiliar to the acquiror the highest-risk option of all has been taken.

To market a new product in the existing market and the same product in a new market are greater risks than they may at first sight seem to be. A new product must automatically sell to a new market to some degree. Even if the market represents substantially the same people, the new product will almost certainly have a different PUV, and to that extent will aim at a different market in that sense. For example, if a car company like Honda attempts to sell lawn-mowers to its existing car buyers, they represent a new market, since Honda has no means of predicting their reaction to its lawn-mowers from its car sales as the two products serve quite different needs. Similarly to sell the same product in a new market means not only understanding a new type of PUV, but also relating to different competitors, and hence probably finding oneself in a totally different position on the Producer Matrix.

At the next level of detail the possible strategic actions can be classified by their appropriate position within the risk cube:

1. Do nothing.
2. Withdraw.
3. Consolidate.
4. Penetrate the existing market.

All fall within the same product/same market box, that is, the bottom left-hand front box. They are each analyzable by using the existing Customer Matrix and Producer Matrix as the basis for considering alternative strategic moves.

Do nothing

As a strategic option this is by no means necessarily an inappropriate strategy in all circumstances. In circumstances where an acceptable level of profit is being achieved, the firm's market share is good, it has a clear sustainable competitive advantage, its product range is still in the growth phase of the product life-cycle and no imminent turbulence in the market can be discerned, the continuance of the existing strategy is clearly correct. However, this should not lead to complacency and a failure to scan the market closely for possible change, and to invest in the development of new products could lead to future problems.

Withdrawal

As a strategy withdrawal is appropriate in a number of circumstances. In a declining market, when a firm's market share is poor and shows little possibility of substantial improvement, a timely withdrawal may minimize future losses. Where the firm has no competitive advantage, and cannot foresee attaining one, it is better to withdraw early than to incur heavy losses and to be forced out later. Other circumstances in which withdrawal is an appropriate strategy are where the resources can be deployed more profitably elsewhere, but only where exit costs are acceptably low. Where they are high, this must be taken into consideration before adopting a withdrawal strategy.

A further set of circumstances are where the industry is strongly cyclical, and withdrawal in order to re-enter later at a better point in the cycle shows good judgement. Thus an astute housing company will build its land bank when prices are at the bottom of the cycle and sell it off when a boom develops, only to repurchase during the next down-swing. Such strategies apply also to foreign exchange, metals, commodities and other speculative industries.

Consolidation

A consolidation strategy involves the reduction of a firm's activities to its profitable core. During the up-swing of a business cycle, a firm is likely to consider expanding into new areas of activity, accepting that they will not necessarily be instantly profitable, but given good judgement and investment should become so in the future. Correspondingly, with the onset of recession, it is appropriate for a firm to consolidate its position in the areas where it has its greatest strength, normally its profitable core business. This involves concentrating its investment in the core areas, and withdrawing from low-profit or unprofitable activities.

Other activities associated with a consolidation strategy are likely to be severe cost-cutting and downsizing, particularly of central overheads, and for the market leader, acquisition at low prices of smaller competitors in order to push market share from strong to dominant. High-capacity utilization is valued in consolidation mode far more than a varied high turnover over a wide range of activities.

Market penetration

As a strategy market penetration is particularly necessary when market growth is slowing, or markets are actually declining. In the event that growth is strong, competitors can achieve fast growth without increasing their market share. However, when the market matures and growth slows, only a strategy of market penetration can enable a firm to increase its sales. Market penetration can be achieved by any combination of Perceived Price reduction and increased Perceived Use Value. Thus the buyer will purchase the firm's product rather than a competitor's, because it is believed to offer better value for money.

Same product/new market

A market development strategy is the next lowest risk to the same product/same market quadrant strategies. This involves constructing a new Customer Matrix relevant to the upper left-hand quadrant on the face of the risk cube. It may also be necessary to reassess the firm's position on the Producer Matrix to determine firstly whether the firm's core competences are those required in this segment, and whether the firm's relative competitive position with regard to its competences and those of competitors operating in this segment are different to those in the base core segment.

A strategy of this kind can be carried out in a variety of ways; firstly, by extending market segments. If, for example, Mercedes is primarily targeted at the over-forty-fives, the easiest and lowest-risk strategy extension is to develop small variants targeted at the thirty-five-year-old. A second possibility is to extend the marketing to new geographical areas. A product sold purely nationally can be extended to the European Community after a little market research to determine acceptable price levels and possible taste differences. A third variant is to discover new uses for existing products, for example the extension of the home games computer to the word-processing personal computer.

New product/same market

The strategy of product development is higher risk than any of the other strategies discussed so far. Whilst overtly only concerned with unfamiliarity in the product area, it is also inevitably operating in a new market area; new, that is, for the product. This strategy will also involve constructing a new Customer Matrix and a new Producer Matrix to determine potential relative competitive strength.

The strategy can be carried out in a number of ways with varying risk:

1. By product range extension.
2. By licensing-in or franchising a new product.
3. By developing a new product through R&D.

Product range extension is the lowest risk of the three strategy variants. The only risk attached to this strategy is of the cannibalization of revenue from the existing product range. This is of course possible, and the risk attached to it increases the further the product range is extended. It is, however, the natural first resort for a firm wishing to increase its sales without changing a winning formula by more than a marginal amount.

The licensing-in of a product or product range has the advantage that the licensed product has by definition been successful in the market of its origin. The risk attached to this strategy is that demand in the prospective licensee's market is different from that in the product's market of origin, and the product will not succeed outside its original home country. The benefit to the licensee is that the product has already been successfully tested from an effectiveness viewpoint, and that no expenditure is needed on R&D. The licensor may even be persuaded to support the product with some marketing expenditure to spread the brand name. Many international products from Coca-Cola to McDonald's have been successfully licensed or franchised to the benefit of both licensor and licensees.

The riskiest product development strategy variant is that based on the firm's own R&D. It is reputed that no more than one in a hundred of R&D developed products is actually successful in a major way. Only companies with a a strong financial position, very strong competence in research and particularly development, and a very effective marketing department should risk embarking on totally new products. In general such a strategy is expensive, very risky and potentially unprofitable.

New product/new market

This strategy should only be adopted in exceptional circumstances, as it is very high risk. Such circumstances might be a new use for an established and potentially market-winning technology in which the firm has a competitive advantage, e.g. the first application of the microchip to the watch market.

The risk cube enables strategists to assess the comparative risk of different options involved in selecting a specific product/market strategy as a means of pursuing a strategic direction on the relevant Customer and Producer Matrices. In general the risk is higher the greater the unfamiliarity of the firm with the challenges facing it. Having considered the various strategies and their attendant risk, the strategist is then faced with the problem of evaluating the strategies in order to make his/her strategic choice.

6.3 Strategy evaluation

Once the firm has considered the possible range of markets and products in which it might compete, it needs to evaluate the various options and select amongst them. When the relative risks of the available strategic options have been considered the options should be evaluated from a number of other viewpoints. These are neatly listed by Johnson and Scholes (1993) as **suitability**, **feasibility** and **acceptability**. It is necessary to score a positive rating under all three of these headings, as well as to be rated as within the company's risk profile, for the strategy to become the chosen one.

Suitability

To be judged suitable, the proposed strategy needs to have a good prospect of achieving the company's proposed financial and other objectives. It also needs to be a strategy that is consistent with the company's mission statement, if any. Thus it must be in an area in which the company wishes to operate, must have a culture not incompatible with the company's ethical philosophy, and if possible must build on the company's strengths, or compensate in some identifiable way for its existing deficiencies.

Thus Ford will have considered whether the launching of the

Scorpio was a suitable strategy. It was launched to compete in the same market segment in which Mercedes, BMW and Lexus are competitors. Under the suitability criterion the questions to be addressed would be the following:

- Would the Scorpio be able to achieve an adequate image positioning to compete effectively in that market segment?
- Would it achieve the market share, overall sales level and profitability to meet Ford's targets?

All selected strategies must pass the suitability test, but of course the individual detailed questions that need to be posed under that head will vary widely from company to company and from situation to situation.

Feasibility

Once the proposed strategy has been judged to be broadly suitable, the question of feasibility needs to be addressed: even if the strategy were chosen, could the company carry it out successfully? The considerations here are whether the company is adequately equipped in terms of financial power, human and other resources, skills, technologies, know-how and organizational strength, that is, core competences to carry out the strategy effectively. If there are doubts on this score it is always possible to consider the possibility of extending the proposed strategy to include one of joint development, with another company or financial institution supplying the deficient resources or competences.

Thus once the Scorpio had been judged likely to meet the company's targets, and to accord with its broader objectives, the next question to be addressed is whether Ford has the competences to manufacture and launch such a quality car. Answering this question would involve a consideration of Ford's recent performance, its competences and its overall image. It may be questioned whether its performance in these areas is to be judged adequate to the task.

One further consideration in assessing feasibility is whether the management team can identify practical first steps that could be taken in order to begin the implementation of the strategy. It is often the absence of a clear view of what the firm would have to do to implement the strategy that exposes the infeasibility of the option.

Acceptability

The third criterion of acceptability addresses the question of whether the company's stakeholders, howsoever defined, would be sufficiently happy with the proposed strategy to give it their support. Generally the larger the company, the greater the number of interests that have to be regarded as stakeholders. Thus in a small owner-managed company, so long as the strategy does not break the law it may be acceptable, as the stakeholders are generally limited to the owner, the employees and the customers. However, for a major multi-national the stakeholder list becomes much longer. The key stakeholders, of course, remain the shareholders, the employees and the customers; but other groups also make their voices heard in relation to the strategies of major corporations: namely, trade unions, the government, the press and often special-interest pressure groups. Although it may be an impossible task to secure the active support of all stakeholder groups in these circumstances, the proposed strategy must at least be acceptable to the central stakeholders, and the possible negative views of the others must be taken into account before the strategy is adopted. In the example, Ford's strategy in relation to the launching of the Scorpio would have had to be acceptable to these stakeholder bodies. If, for example, Ford had already owned Jaguar when they proposed to launch the Scorpio, the Jaguar management might have found the launch unacceptable and opposed it, since it could be judged to compete directly with Jaguar's products, as well as with Mercedes, BMW and Lexus.

Strategy options should initially be considered from the viewpoint of risk. In general the further they require the company to stray from the business area in which it has built its reputation the greater the risk. A riskier strategy should not be adopted if a less risky one would achieve the chosen objectives equally well. When the risk test has been applied the proposed strategy should then be tested for its ability to meet objectives (suitability), the company's capacity to carry it out successfully (feasibility) and the acceptability of the strategy to the stakeholders.

6.4 A worked example

Consider a firm, called say Teklato, in a small segment of the synthetic-textiles industry. It has one product that dominates its segment and is patented, but the patent has only two years to run. The company has developed a new product that is an improvement on the old one, and is billed to replace it, as the old product replaced its predecessor ten years earlier, when its patent was about to run out. Teklato has a strong tradition of high-quality R&D, and has invented many products that it has subsequently licensed abroad. The product is extruded from ICI raw material. However, although ICI's prices for the raw material have been rising steadily over the years, Teklato has not felt able to pass on these price rises to customers, and declining profit margins have resulted.

Teklato appears on the Customer Matrix as medium-priced and with a high PUV, which position starts to decline on both axes as the patent comes to an end. On the Producer Matrix, Teklato is only fairly well up the effectiveness axis, since its only real core competence is its R&D capacity. It does not rate well on the cost efficiency axis, so it is vulnerable in the future.

Three possible strategies are considered:

1. Phase out the old product as its patent ends, and phase in the new patented product.

2. Concentrate on the R&D function and licensing, selling the production unit to a management buy-out.

3. Reconfigure the activity cost chain, keeping an integrated company but forming an alliance with a strong marketing company that lacks a production arm.

All three strategies move very little out of the home quadrant, although strategy 3 involves greater risk than the other two, since it has an alliance at its core, rather than internal development.

In order to select the preferred strategy, the three factors of suitability, feasibility and acceptability need to be considered. They may be applied as follows. Strategy 3 scores highest on suitability, as it is likely to give the best sales and profit results. The combination of a strong marketing company with Teklato's adequate production and strong R&D, give it a powerful position on the Producer Matrix, which should feed through to a strong position on the Customer Matrix. The licensing option has limited potential for profit, and the strategy to replace the old product with the new may not work without stronger marketing.

On the question of feasibility, more work would need to be done. The questions need to be answered of whether a management buy-out is possible, and whether an interested strong marketing company can be found with which to form an alliance. Strategy 1 is probably feasible as something similar has been done earlier.

The question of stakeholder acceptability also needs to be addressed to the stakeholders. No doubt strategy 1 is acceptable as it involves little change from current operations. As regards strategies 2 and 3, however, it is important to discover the stakeholders' views on splitting the company between the R&D function and the rest, and alternatively allying with a marketing company, and thus having to share the potentially larger profit. When these questions were successfully resolved the preferred strategy would emerge.

6.5 Summary

A company's initial concern must be to achieve as strong as possible a position in the Customer Matrix of its existing products and markets, based on strong cost efficiency and effectiveness competences on its Producer Matrix. If this proves impossible, it will need to consider the higher-risk options of moving to different markets, and/or possibly different products. These moves involve higher risk, since they mean moving into unfamiliar territory.

The questions of whether to make the moves by internal development, by alliance or by acquisition also need to be considered, since all but internal development also involve the unfamiliar, and thus involve a raising of the company's risk profile. When the identified options have been analyzed and compared, the choice of the preferred option can be made by rating each option against the criteria of suitability, feasibility and acceptability. The preferred option needs to rate acceptably highly when measured against all three criteria.

7

Joint development and acquisition

The firm needs to decide at this stage how to put together the necessary resources and competences to have a chance of achieving competitive advantage in its selected product markets. There are only three possible answers to the question 'How?':

1. By joint development.
2. By acquisition.
3. By internal development.

This chapter considers the advantages and disadvantages of joint development and of acquisition.

Some form of alliance with a partner overcomes many of the problems of lack of resources and competences. New products from one company can be married to sales forces with spare capacity from another, and the time from product to market dramatically shortened. Companies strong on technology can collaborate with partners strong on marketing to their mutual benefit. The wide variety of joint development forms provides a varied menu of possibilities for partners to select from, to optimize their development potentials.

Joint development is appropriate where sustainable competitive advantage can be achieved together but not separately. A weak position on the Producer Matrix can be transformed through an alliance by the addition of the partner's core competences. Joint venture, collaboration and consortium are the principal types of alliance to meet differing situational and firm needs. Other less committing and interdependent forms of joint development include one-off projects, licensing, franchising and the appointment of exclusive agents. These are unilateral arrangements implying only limited interdependence between the cooperating firms.

Figure 7.1 illustrates some general circumstances in which joint development or an alliance may be most appropriate. In the normal situation of relative resource and competence limitations, where particular individual activities are of little strategic importance, the firm should buy them in, even if it can produce them itself with an efficiency comparable to the best in the industry. This will release resources for the company to concentrate its activities in areas which have at least medium strategic importance, and where it is at least moderately competent by comparison with the industry's best. It should concentrate investment on areas of high strategic importance where it is only moderately competent.

This leaves three areas where joint development or alliance is the optimal way to develop. These areas are where the activity is of medium or high strategic importance, but the firm has a low level of competence in it, and thirdly where it is of medium strategic importance and the firm's competence compared with the best in the industry is only medium. In these circumstances, an alliance will be most appropriate if a partner can be found with complementary competences and needs.

Joint development has risks attached, however. Know-how will inevitably leak intentionally and often unintentionally to a partner, who may become a future competitor. Joint development means working with new people and learning new ways of doing things,

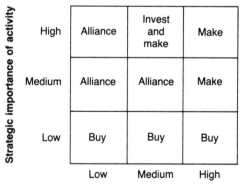

Competence compared with the best in the industry

Figure 7.1 The Make/Buy/Ally Matrix

which can take time, lead to cultural problems and incur additional costs of coordination. Finally, in a joint development arrangement, there is an inevitable lack of clarity of authority, which may be a disadvantage when confronted with an internally developed rival with clear lines of decision-making.

7.1   Cooperative strategy

Cooperative strategy is rapidly becoming the counterpart to competitive strategy as a key strategic management tool. It is perhaps the primary means for companies, deficient in certain competences or resources, to link with others with complementary skills and resources to give them jointly competitive advantage, particularly in the increasingly globalizing world markets. It also has the added advantage of flexibility in a volatile world.

The stimulus for cooperative strategy

It is probably unhelpful, however, to think of cooperation as the opposite of competition, since firms generally cooperate with each other only in order to harness the resources, skills and power to compete more effectively with others in the marketplace. The issue, then, is not 'To compete or to cooperate' but rather how best to organize the appropriate set of resources and competences to become a winner in the competitive marketplace. And since more marketplaces are becoming global, the critical mass of resources needed to succeed is growing faster than many internally developed companies can cope with alone. Thus the resource-based approach to strategy development described in Chapter 3 above may lead a company to identify competences that it needs if it is to succeed. Cooperation with another company is one way of meeting these needs.

In a growing number of areas, a careful consideration of the appropriate make-or-buy options for particular company activities may lead many manufacturers to opt to become mere assemblers, or even purely brand-marketing companies; or medium-sized companies may become global enterprises almost overnight by setting up a wide network of strategic alliances to meet global challenges and opportunities.

The movement of enterprises away from a simple wholly owned corporate structure to more federated forms is accentuated by the growth of alliances, and other strategic networks, which aid the development of global loyalties and cooperative endeavours quite distinct from those encouraged by the old national and firm boundaries.

Organizational forms are conventionally described on a scale of increasing integration with markets at one end as the absolute of non-integration, to hierarchies or completely integrated companies at the other. It is often suggested that the organizations that survive are those that involve the lowest costs to run in the particular circumstances in which they exist. Thus integrated companies will be the lowest cost in situations when assets are very specific, markets are thin, and where conditions are highly complex and uncertain. Such conditions would make the fully integrated form of organization the most appropriate one, as it would be very difficult and therefore costly to handle transactions in a fragmented market-place way.

At the other extreme, transactions are best carried out in markets where no one deal implies commitment to another, and relationships are completely arm's length. This is most commonly the case when the product is a frequently traded commodity, assets are not specific, market pricing is needed for efficiency, there are many alternative sources of supply and the costs of running a company would be very high. Thus few companies needing nails occasionally, but without their being critical and in scarce supply, would manufacture them. They would buy them in the market.

Between the extremes of markets and integrated companies, there is a range of interorganizational forms of increasing levels of integration which have evolved to deal with varying circumstances and, where they survive, may be assumed to do so as a result of their varying appropriateness to the situation as organizational forms, as shown in Figure 7.2. All forms short of those to the top and the bottom of the triangle exhibit some degree of cooperation in their activities. Thus arm's-length market relationships may develop into those with established suppliers and distributors, and then may integrate further into loose cooperative networks.

Further up the ladder of integration come the hub-subcontractor networks like Marks and Spencers' close interrelationships with its suppliers. Licensing agreements come next, in which the relationship between the licensor and the licensee is integrated from the viewpoint of activities in a defined area, but both retain their separate ownership and identities.

Between licensing agreements and completely integrated companies, where rule by price (markets) is replaced by rule by fiat

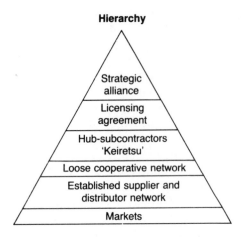

Figure 7.2   There are many intermediate organizational forms between
markets and hierarchies

(companies), comes the most integrated form of rule by cooperation, namely that found in strategic alliances.

Alliances may be preferred organizational forms where sensitive market awareness is required, the price mechanism remains important, risks of information leakage are not considered unacceptably high, scale economies and finance risks are high, there is resource limitation and flexibility is important.

These diverse forms of cooperative agreements are sometimes called unilateral or bilateral. Unilateral agreements are so called because they typically involve minimal amounts of partner interdependence. Examples of unilateral agreements would be technical training, supplier contracts, franchising, patent licensing or a marketing consultancy. The agreements have quite specific tasks, and each partner could terminate the agreement without great cost. Generally the relationship is a purely financial one.

Strategic alliances are bilateral agreements, and involve a larger amount of interdependence. They include non-equity cooperative agreements, equity joint ventures and consortia, and involve the partners tying their fortunes together to a much greater extent than in unilateral arrangements.

In the consideration of cooperative strategy a number of issues need to be addressed:

1.   Why do firms cooperate?
2.   How do they select their partners?

3. What are the principal forms of cooperation?
4. How are such arrangements best managed?
5. What happens to cooperative arrangements in the long term?

This chapter will consider these issues in turn.

7.2   Why do firms cooperate?

Cooperative relationships develop normally because a firm develops a feeling that it is deficient in certain important competences. Companies with weak positions on the Customer Matrix, reflecting equally weak positions on the Producer Matrix, seek partners to strengthen their core competences and improve their competitive position. Realization by a firm that it is in such a position often comes about as a result of the growth in strength of an external force that starts to concern it, often causing its financial or market performance to decline.

External forces

There are a number of external forces, that have stimulated the growth of strategic alliances in recent years. Amongst the most important are the globalization of tastes and markets, the rapid spread and shortening life-cycle of new technology and its products, the development of opportunities for achieving major economies of scale, scope and learning, increasing turbulence in international economies, a heightened level of uncertainty in all aspects of life and declining international trade barriers.

Globalization of tastes
Theodore Levitt was credited over twenty years ago with first having drawn attention to the increasing homogenization of tastes, leading to the development of the 'global village'. Since that time the globalization movement has spread to an increasing number of industries, and it is now possible to travel from New York to Paris and on to Tokyo, and to see very similar articles on display in department stores in all three cities.

After the Second World War, trade barriers between nations placed a limit to the development of a world economy. With the dramatic economic recovery of the major combatant nations, particularly Germany and Japan, the move towards increasing international trade was stimulated by international agreements to reduce trade barriers and thus increase overall economic welfare, by allowing greater specialization on the basis of comparative costs.

GATT, the European Union, EFTA and other trading agreements and common markets enabled national firms to develop opportunities internationally, and to grow into multi-nationals. More recently the 1992 EU legislation, the reunification of Germany, the establishment of NAFTA and the break-up of the communist bloc have accelerated this movement, and in so doing have stimulated the growth of strategic alliances between firms in different nations.

Global technology

The most modern technologies, namely micro-electronics, genetic engineering and advanced material sciences are by now all subject to truly global competition. The global technologies involved in the communications revolution have also succeeded in effect in 'shrinking' the world, and have led to the design and manufacture of products with global appeal, due to their pricing, reliability and technical qualities. But not only is technology becoming global in nature, it is also changing faster than previously, which means a single firm needs correspondingly greater resources to be capable of replacing the old technology with the new on a regular basis. This is often difficult to finance and resource.

Economies of scale and scope

The globalization of markets and technologies leads to the need to be able to produce at a sufficiently large volume to realize the maximum economies of scale and scope, and thus compete globally on a unit cost basis. Although one effect of the new technologies is, through flexible manufacturing systems, to be able to produce small lots economically, the importance of scale and scope economies is still critical to global economic competitiveness. Alliances are often the only way to achieve such a large scale of operation to generate these economies. The advantages of alliances and networks over integrated firms are in the areas of specialization, entrepreneurship and flexibility of arrangements, and these characteristics are particularly appropriate to meet the needs of today's turbulent and changing environment.

Growing turbulence

The oil crises of 1973 and 1978, the Middle East wars and the subsequent aggravated economic cycles of boom and recession, coupled with ever shortening product life-cycles, have made economic forecasting as hazardous as long-term weather forecasting. Strategic vulnerability due to environmental uncertainty has become a fact of life in most industries. Cooperative strategy helps to reduce that vulnerability, by enabling 'cooperative enterprises' to grow or decline flexibly, to match the increasing variability of the market situation.

Internal conditions

A range of external conditions may stimulate the creation of strategic alliances. However, firms will only enter into such arrangements when their internal circumstances make this seem to be the right move. These internal circumstances have most commonly included a feeling of resource and competence inadequacy, in that an alliance would give a firm access to valuable markets, technologies, special skills or raw materials in which it feels itself to be deficient, and which it could not easily get in any other way.

Other internal circumstances that have stimulated the search for alliances have included the belief that running an alliance would be cheaper than running and financing an integrated company, or the belief that an alliance, or a series of alliances, would provide strong protection against take-over predators. Still others may be that firms believe it is the best way to limit risk, or to achieve a desired market position faster than by any other way.

Competence inadequacy

The theory of competence inadequacy suggests that the crucial condition determining the survival of a firm is not its competitive advantage but its access to resources and competences. Thus if a highly competitive firm overtrades – that is, runs out of resources – it fails to survive; on the other hand, if a sleepy firm is part of a very large and indulgent conglomerate, it can survive as long as its parent considers it worth supplying with the necessary resources.

In conditions of economic turbulence and high uncertainty, access to the necessary resources becomes at risk, which raises the spectre of potential strategic vulnerability for even the most efficient firm. This leads to the need to reduce that uncertainty, and secure a more reliable access to the necessary resources, whether they be supplies, skills or markets. Strategic alliances with firms able to supply the resources may then develop where previously market relationships may have dominated.

There are many forms of resource dependency:

Access to markets is a common form. One firm has a successful product in its home market, but lacks the sales force and perhaps the local knowledge to gain access to other markets. The alliance between Cincinnati Bell Information Systems of the United States and Kingston Communications of Hull, England, was set up from CBIS's viewpoint in order to gain market access into the European Community, with the purpose of selling its automated telecommunications equipment. The market motivator is also a strong one in the current spate of Eastern Europe and former Soviet alliances with Western firms.

Access to technology is another form of resource need. Thus in forming Cereal Partners to fight Kellogg's domination of the breakfast cereals market, Nestlé has joined forces with General Mills principally to gain access to its breakfast cereals technology and its marketing skills.

Access to special skills is a similar form of resource need to access to technology. The special skills or competences may be of many types, and include the know-how associated with experience in a particular product area.

Access to raw materials is a further form. Thus, for example, Monarch Resources has allied with Cyprus Minerals to gain access to Venezuelan gold mines. Although this motivation was a very common one in past decades, when the developed nations sought allies in less developed areas, it is less common currently.

Costs
Although accurate calculation of the costs involved in various organizational forms is very difficult to compute, since it involves adding the quantitative and the qualitative costs, the lowest-cost concept is still valuable in determining whether a particular activity is best carried out by internal means, by purchasing it in the market or by collaboration with a partner. This is reflected on the efficiency axis of the Producer Matrix.

Risk limitation

Alliances are frequently formed as a result of the need to limit risk. The nature of the risk may be its sheer size in terms of financial resources. Thus a £100 million project shared between three alliance partners is a much lower risk for each partner than the same project shouldered alone. The risk may also be portfolio risk. Thus £100 million invested in alliances in four countries probably represents a lower risk than the same figure invested alone in one project. The trade-off is between higher control and lower risk. An acquisition represents a high level of control but is expensive, and however well the acquiror may have researched the target company before purchase, it may still receive some unexpected surprises after the conclusion of the deal. A strategic alliance involves shared risk, is probably easier to unravel if it proves disappointing, and enables the partners to get to know each other slowly, as their relationship develops.

Speed to market

The need to achieve speed is a further internal reason for alliance formation. Many an objective in the business world of the 1990s can be achieved only if the firm acts quickly. In many industries there is a need for almost instantaneous product launches in the retail markets of London, Tokyo and New York if 'windows of opportunity' are not to be missed. This suggests the need for alliances, which can be activated rapidly to take advantage of such opportunities.

Defence against predators

Alliances are not all formed with expansionary aims in mind, however. Many are the result of fear of being taken over. Thus in the European insurance world AXA and Groupe Midi of France formed an alliance and eventually merged to avoid being taken over by Generali of Italy. General Electric of the United Kingdom has formed an alliance with its namesake in the United States for similar defensive reasons.

7.3   Partner selection

The creation of a strategic alliance does not of course guarantee its long-term survival. Research by the consultancy firms McKinsey, and Coopers and Lybrands has shown that there is no better than a

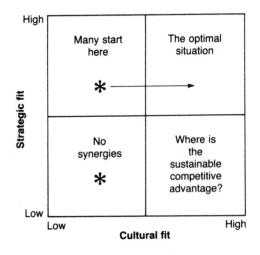

Figure 7.3   The best alliances should aim for both strategic and cultural fit

50 per cent survival probability for alliances over a five-year term. This conclusion is, however, put in perspective when considered against Porter's (1987) research into the success of acquisitions, which concluded that this route to growth was little better in terms of probable successful outcome.

One of the keys to a successful alliance must be to choose the right partner. This requires the consideration of two basic factors:

1.   The synergy or strategic fit between the partners.
2.   The cultural fit between them.

The importance of strategic fit and cultural fit can be illustrated in Figure 7.3. A high degree of strategic fit is essential to justify the alliance in the first place. Strategic fit implies that the core competences of the two companies are highly complementary. However, for the alliance to endure, cultural adaptation must take place, leading the most successful alliances to graduate to the top right-hand box.

Strategic fit

Strategic fit, of some form or another, is normally the fundamental reason that the alliance has been set up in the first place. It is important both that it is clearly there at the outset, and that it continues to exist for the lifetime of the alliance. Strategic fit implies that the alliance has developed or is capable of developing a clearly identifiable source of sustainable competitive advantage.

Whatever partner is sought, it must be one with complementary assets, that is, to supply some of the resource or competences needed to achieve the alliance objectives. These complementary needs may come about in a number of circumstances:

Legal necessity: this may be brought about by the legal requirement, particularly in many developing countries, that international companies take a local partner before being granted permission to trade.

Reciprocity: the assets of the two partners have a reciprocal strength, that is, there are synergies such that a newly configured joint value chain leads to greater power than the two companies could hope to exercise separately.

Efficiency: where an alliance leads to lower joint costs over an important range of areas – scale, scope, transaction, procurement and so forth, then this provides a powerful stimulus to alliance formation.

Reputation: alliances are set up to create a more prestigious enterprise with a higher profile in the marketplace, enhanced image, prestige and reputation.

For cooperation to be appropriate, both partners should need and be able to provide some resource or competence the other possesses. If the needs are not reciprocal, then the best course of action is for the partner in need to buy the competence or resource, or if appropriate buy the company possessing it. Cooperative arrangements require the satisfaction of complementary needs on the part of both partners, and thereby lead to competitive advantage.

Cultural fit

Cultural fit is an expression more difficult to define than strategic fit. In the sense used here, it covers the following factors. The partners have cultural sensitivities sufficiently acute and flexible to be able to work effectively together, and to learn from each other's cultural differences. The partners are balanced in the sense of being of roughly equivalent size, strength and consciousness of need. One is not therefore likely to attempt to dominate the other. Also their attitude to risk and to ethical considerations is compatible.

7.4   Alliance formation

Having found an appropriate partner, the new allies are faced with the question of how to form an alliance in the most appropriate way. Alliances can usefully be classified along three dimensions that define their nature, form and membership:

1. Focused ————————————————————— Complex
2. Joint venture ————————————————— Collaboration
3. Two partners only ————————————— Consortium

Figure 7.4 illustrates the options available from which a choice may be made.

Focused alliances

The focused alliance is an arrangement between two or more companies, set up to meet a clearly defined set of circumstances in a particular way. It normally involves for each partner only one major activity or function, or at least is clearly defined and limited in its objectives. Thus, for example, a US company seeking to enter the EU market with a given set of products may form an alliance with a European distribution company as its means of market entry. The US company provides the product, and probably some market and sales literature, and the European company provides the sales force and local know-how. The precise form of arrangement may vary widely, but the nature of the alliance is a focused one with clear remits and understandings of respective contributions and rewards.

Complex alliances

Complex alliances may involve the complete activity cost chains of the partners. The companies recognize that together, potentially, they form a far more powerful competitive enterprise than they do apart; yet they wish to retain their separate identities and overall

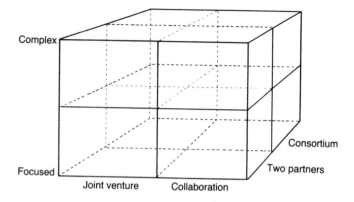

Eight types of strategic alliance combination

1. Focused/complex.
2. Joint venture or collaboration.
3. Two partners or consortium.

Figure 7.4   The strategic alliance options

aspirations, whilst being willing to cooperate with each other over a wide range of activities. Rover/Honda is a good example of a complex alliance. Currently it includes joint R&D, joint manufacturing, joint development and sourcing of parts. It remains separate, however, in the critical marketing and sales areas, and both companies retain clearly distinct images. The alliance, prior to BMW's purchase of Rover from British Aerospace, involved a 20 per cent share exchange between Rover and Honda's UK manufacturing company. Alliances that begin focused often develop into the complex form if they are successful.

Joint ventures

Joint ventures involve the creation of a legally separate company from that of the partners. The new company normally starts life with the partners as its shareholders, and with an agreed set of objectives in a specific area of activity. Thus a US company may set up a joint venture with a UK company to market in the European Community. The partners provide finance and other support competences and resources for the joint venture in agreed amounts. The aim of the joint venture is normally that the new company should ultimately become a self-standing entity with its own employees and strategic aims, quite distinct from those of its parent shareholders. Unilever is a good example of a joint venture set up by a Dutch and an English company in the 1920s, and which has grown into a major multi-national enterprise. Joint ventures usually involve non-core activities of the partners, and are characterized by having clear boundaries, specific assets, personnel and managerial responsibilities. Ultimately they are divestible by the partners in a way that the non-joint venture form is not.

Collaborations

The collaborative alliance form is employed when partners do not wish to set up a separate joint venture company to provide boundaries to their relationship. This might be because they do not know at the outset where such boundaries should lie; hence the more flexible collaborative form meets their needs better. Collaborative alliances are also preferred when the partners' core business is the area of the alliances, and therefore assets cannot be separated from the core business and allocated to a dedicated joint venture. The collaborative form can be expanded or contracted to meet the partners' needs far more easily than can a joint venture. Rover/Honda is a classic example of the collaboration form of alliance.

The consortium

The consortium is a distinct form of strategic alliance in that it has a number of partners, and is normally a very large-scale activity set up for a very specific purpose, and usually managed in a hands-off fashion from the contributing shareholders. Consortia are particularly common for large-scale projects in the defence or aerospace industries, where massive funds and a wide range of specialist competences are required for success. Airbus Industrie is a consortium where a number of European shareholders have set up an aircraft manufacturing company to compete on world markets with Boeing and McDonnell Douglas. The European shareholders, although large themselves, felt the need to create a large enough pool of funds to ensure they reached critical mass in terms of resources for aircraft development, and chose to form an international consortium to do this.

There are then eight possible basic configurations of alliance covering the alliance's nature, its form and the number of partners it has, for example, a focused, joint venture with two partners, a complex collaboration, consortium and so forth. The alliance type that involves setting up a joint venture company is currently by far the most popular method. There are also well-trodden paths by which alliances evolve: for example, focused alliances that are successful frequently develop into complex alliances, as the partners find other areas for mutual cooperation. Two-partner alliances often recruit further partners, and develop into consortia, as the scale and complexity of opportunities become apparent. Alliances, initially without joint venture companies, frequently form them subsequently, as they experience difficulty in operating in a partially merged fashion, but without clear boundaries between the cooperative and the independent parts. It is also quite common for one partner in a joint venture to buy out the other. This need not mean the alliance was a failure: it may have been a considerable success, but the strategic objectives of the two companies may have moved onto different paths.

Other paths of evolution, however, are probably less likely to be followed. Consortia are unlikely to reduce to two-partner alliances. Alliances with joint venture companies are unlikely to revert to a non-joint venture situation, but to keep the alliance in being. Thirdly, complex alliances are unlikely to revert to a simple focused relationship between the partners.

It is not possible to predict definitively which form of cooperative agreement will be adopted in which specific set of circumstances, since certain companies show policy preferences for certain forms rather than others, irrespective of their appropriateness. Most cooperative agreements may be classified into four types:

1. Two-partner joint ventures.
2. Two-partner collaborations.
3. Consortium joint ventures.
4. Collaborative networks.

Firms seeking cooperative arrangements generally choose between these four forms, before moving on to define their relationships in a more specific way.

7.5   The management of a cooperative agreement

The management of an alliance consists of two primary factors:

1. The **attitudes** of the partners towards each other.
2. The **mechanisms** chosen to operate the alliance.

Although the mechanisms chosen will obviously vary widely according to the alliance form chosen, the attitudes necessary for success are similar in all forms of alliance.

Attitudes of the partners

The relationship of the partners, as in a marriage, is a key to the success of the arrangement. It may not be a sufficient factor by itself, since the successful alliance needs positive quantifiable results, but it is certainly a necessary condition. An appropriate attitude has two major components, commitment and trust.

● Lack of **commitment** can kill an alliance in a very short time. When the Rover/Honda alliance was set up in 1979 commentators were concerned lest Rover's commitment to it was not matched equally by that of Honda. Rover's economic survival depended upon the alliance and its commitment has been high from the outset. The alliance was less important from Honda's viewpoint; however, the Japanese company has shown an equal degree of commitment throughout and the alliance has been a very successful one. Other alliances have failed because the partners have not allocated their best people to the project, have placed it low on the priority agenda or have set up too many alliances in the hope that at least some would succeed. These attitudes have the seeds of failure within them.

● **Trust** is the second key factor for survival. Unless this develops early on in the partnership the alliance soon ceases to be the best organizational arrangement for the partners, as they spend increasing amounts of time and resources monitoring each other's activities as a result of their mutual lack of trust. Trust does not imply naive revelation of company secrets not covered by the alliance agreement. It implies the belief that the partner will act with integrity, and will carry out its commitments. The appropriate attitude must be set from the start. During the negotiation stage, friendliness should be exhibited, and a deal struck that is clearly 'win–win'; qualities quite different from those that often characterize take-over negotiations.

Goal compatibility is vital to the long-term success of a partnership. Of course the specific goals of the alliance will evolve over time; however, if the goals of the partners fundamentally clash, the alliance cannot but be a short-term opportunistic affair. Compatibility does not necessarily mean the partners' goals must be identical. Rover's current goals are to be an up-market niche player in the automobile industry; Honda has more ambitious goals of global success over a wide product range. There is, however, no fundamental incompatibility in this.

Cultural fit can be analyzed under two headings: basic cultural compatibility and cultural sensitivity.

- **Cultural compatibility** does not necessarily imply the existence of similar cultures. Indeed partners have more to learn from differences than from similarities. It does, however, require a willingness to display cultural sensitivity, and to accept that there is often more than one acceptable way of doing things. A comparison of the partners' cultural webs (see Chapter 4 above) will often highlight possible areas of future cultural discord.
- **Cultural sensitivity** can also be the key to alliance success. Many an alliance has failed purely as a result of cultural incompatibility. The major problem between AT&T and Olivetti probably stemmed from a clash between the contrasting cultures of a bureaucratic US giant corporation in AT&T, and an entrepreneurial Italian marketing company in Olivetti. This may lead to difficulty in working together, to mistrust and ultimately to a growing scepticism as to whether the strategic synergy was there in the first place.

Mechanisms for alliance management

The mechanisms for running a joint venture are quite distinct from those of a collaboration. A joint venture, whether two-partner or consortium, involves, by definition, the creation of a separate company from those of the partners. There are therefore two types of relationship to cope with: the relationship between the partners, and that between each partner and the joint venture company. In a sense, the most appropriate systems for running a joint venture are also the simplest. The venture should be set up with sufficient resources, guaranteed assistance by the partners whilst it is young, and allowed to get on with the job of realizing its objectives and targets. Involvement by the partners should be limited to board level, except at the request of the venture company. A chief executive should be appointed and given sufficient autonomy to build the joint venture company. Although this seems common sense, it is surprising how many joint ventures falter or fail through the unwillingness of the partners to give them sufficient autonomy and assets, and to realize that the venture will inevitably not have objectives fully congruent with those of the partners. Joint venture companies inevitably develop cultures, lives and objectives of their own, and owner partners frequently find this fact difficult to adjust to.

The relationship between the partners is different in nature from that between partners in collaborations. Here the 'boundary-spanning' mechanism is the area crucial for success. The interface between the companies is the area where culture clashes, or conflict of objectives, will probably show themselves first. The establishment of a 'gateway' executive or office, as a channel for all contacts between the partners at least during the settling-down period of the alliance, is a good way to avoid unnecessary misunderstandings.

In all circumstances, a good dispute resolution mechanism should be established before the alliance begins to operate. If this is left to be worked out as necessary, the risk that its absence will lead to a souring of the relationship between the partners at the ultra-sensitive early stage of the partnership is too high to risk.

An effective system for disseminating alliance information widely within the partner companies is a further important factor for ensuring that both or all partners gain in learning to the greatest degree possible from the cooperative arrangement.

Finally a procedure in the event of a wish by either party to end the alliance should be agreed at the outset, since this will increase the feeling of security by both parties that an end to the alliance does not represent a potential catastrophe.

7.6 Alliance evolution

A key factor in the life of an alliance seems to be that if it ceases to evolve, it starts to decay. The reality of a successful alliance is that it not only trades competences but also demonstrates synergies. Whereas the Resource Dependency Perspective (Pfeffer and Salancik 1978) identifies a key part of a company's motivation for forming an alliance, the successful evolution of that alliance depends upon the realization of synergies between the companies, and the establishment of a sustainable competitive advantage for the partners that each could not as easily realize alone.

Important conditions for evolution include the following:

1. Perception of balanced benefits from the alliance by both partners.
2. The development of strong bonding factors.
3. The regular development of new projects between the partners.
4. The adoption of a philosophy of constant learning by the partners.

The comparison cited above of an alliance with a marriage is a very relevant one. Western marriages could be regarded as unstable, as they currently have a high failure rate. In fact they have many of the qualities of strategic alliances. The partners retain separate identities but collaborate over a whole range of activities. Stability is threatened if one partner becomes excessively dependent on the other, or if the benefits are perceived to be all one way. But none the less, successful marriages are stable, and for the same reason as successful alliances. They depend upon trust, commitment, mutual learning, flexibility and a feeling by both partners that they are stronger together than apart. Many businesses point to the need to negotiate decisions in alliances as a weakness, in contrast to companies, where hierarchies make decisions. This is to confuse stability with clarity of decision-making, and would lead to the suggestion that dictatorships are more stable than democracies.

In this analogy, it is commitment to the belief that the alliance represents the best available arrangement that is the foundation of its stability. The need for resolution of the inevitable tensions in such an arrangement can as easily be presented as a strength, rather than as an inherent problem. It leads to the need to debate, to see and evaluate and to reconcile contrasting viewpoints.

Strategic alliances and other forms of cooperative strategy are now widely recognized as appropriate interorganizational forms to meet certain environmental and internal firm conditions. They have distinctive characteristics, such as speed of creation, flexibility, opportunities for specialization, access to additional resources and risk limitation, that make them attractive when compared with the alternatives of internal development, acquisition or market purchases.

This is particularly the case in volatile, uncertain environments, where the need to negotiate some resource security and to develop a rapid global presence become of paramount importance to the survival of the firm, and the development of competitive advantage in a world increasingly dominated by multi-nationals. Cooperative strategy is therefore not an alternative to competitive strategy, but is a means of achieving sustainable competitive advantage, the better to pursue competitive strategy in relation to rivals outside the alliance.

7.7   Acquisitions

Of the 'how?' strategies, the option of acquisition is by far the riskiest, unless pursued after an extended period of close collaboration with the target company as a partner. As a means of effecting a competitive strategy, it is generally pursued for the same reasons as alliances: to get access to core competences in which the acquiring company feels itself to be deficient. Clearly acquisitions are undertaken for other reasons of **corporate** strategy, such as achieving a 'balanced' portfolio of businesses. In this book, however, we are limiting our discussion to the role acquisitions can play in developing **competitive** strategy.

Acquisition has some advantages over both internal development and alliances, of course, which make it such a popular strategy for an ambitious company intent on fast growth:

1. It enables a firm to get rapidly into new market or product areas, and if the acquisition is at an attractive price, and the acquired management team is willing genuinely to transfer their allegiance to the acquiror company, can clearly lead to a new and strengthened enlarged enterprise.

2. It may also enable costs to be reduced through rationalization and the consequent economies of scale and of scope.

3. It may bring valuable skills and resources to the acquiring company, thereby strengthening its core competences and improving its competitive position.

4. By acquiring a competitor the company may improve its market share and put itself in a stronger market position.

However, there are frequently major risks attached to acquisitions, against which the buyer must guard very carefully:

1. The business equivalent of Catch 22 often applies. If the price is low and represents a discount on asset value, the company may be a weak one, and would represent a poor purchase, likely to absorb management time and weaken the acquiror. If the company is a good one, however, the price is likely to be correspondingly high, which will mean the addition of a large amount of goodwill to the acquiror's balance sheet, and an initial decline in return on capital until some synergies can be realized and caused to feed through to profits.

2. A further problem is valuation. A shrewd seller will of course dress up the company's accounts to reflect it in the most profitable light to achieve the best price. Such profits and asset values may turn out not to be sustainable after the purchase has been completed.

3. The best of the acquired company's personnel may have left by the time the new owner takes over, and if the acquired company was largely owner-managed, the former owners may be less highly motivated on becoming employees.

4. Company cultures may be found to clash and the process of achieving the promised synergies may prove more difficult than seemed apparent during the acquisition appraisal process.

It is important, therefore, if an acquisition strategy is to be adopted, to pursue it in a methodical low-risk way, noting certain key factors before proceeding; for instance, an acquisition can in general be justified only if it leaves the combined enterprise stronger than the sum of the two individual enterprises. This normally means that both parties should be able to bring something to the party, in the same way that is expected from an alliance. The requirement that the joint value chains of the acquiring and the acquired company be able to achieve a sustainable competitive advantage that is not easily attainable by either party separately, applies to acquisitions as well as to alliances. It therefore requires the possession of complementary assets, and of realizable synergies between the two parties. An acquisition made principally to increase the size of a portfolio, and not able to achieve, for example, economies of scale or scope, is therefore of doubtful value as a strategic move.

The following eight-step approach is suggested as a route to minimizing acquisition risks:

1. Rule out acquisitions in industries and fields unrelated to those with which the acquiror has experience, and which seem to require skills and competences that the acquiror does not have. Michael Porter's research (1987) into the record of acquisitions made in areas unrelated to the core competences or experience of the acquiring company shows a failure rate between 61 and 74 per cent (see Figure 7.5).

2. Conduct an internal appraisal of your own business, including value chain analysis, core competence profiling and a resource audit. Estimate the financial worth of your company, identify the nature and strength of your claim to sustainable competitive advantage, and the breadth of product market segments in which it applies.

3. Select a small number of industry sectors for initial investigation to search for appropriate acquisition candidates. The selection of sectors should be based on criteria following from a chosen strategic approach to development. Hanson, for example, selects industry sectors based on the criteria that they are mature, do not require large R&D expenditure, are not high-technology and have within them established companies with strong brand names but low price/earnings valuations. The sectors should also mesh closely, in their required key competences, with the company's existing core competences, so that there will not be too many surprises in the acquired company's environment.

4. Select criteria for acquisition candidates and divide them into 'must haves' and 'nice to haves': for example, a 'must have' criterion might be existing strong and committed management, and a 'nice to have' criterion might be a large market share, or *vice versa*. The selection of the criteria depends upon the carefully thought-out requirements of the acquiring company.

5. Identify potential candidates that meet the criteria within the selected industry sectors. Having done so, the value chains and

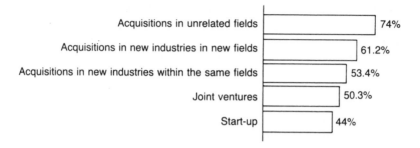

Acquisitions in unrelated fields 74%
Acquisitions in new industries in new fields 61.2%
Acquisitions in new industries within the same fields 53.4%
Joint ventures 50.3%
Start-up 44%

Definitions
● A field is a sector. Thus a bank acquiring a property company is entering a new field.
● A new industry is a narrower definition, for instance a bank acquiring an insurance company; both are within the financial services field.

(adapted from Porter 1987)

Figure 7.5 The failure rate of acquisitions in the USA is high

competence profiles of the acquiring and would-be acquired companies should be compared to identify potential complementarities and synergies.

6. The candidates should then be investigated further to determine their ownership, track record, potential problems and possible risk areas. Approximate acquisition values should then be assigned to them at this stage.

7. Once an appropriate candidate has been identified and contacted and has shown interest, a careful and rigorous 'due diligence' process, including the real reason for interest in a possible sale, must be carried out if unpleasant surprises are to be avoided.

8. Once the negotiations have been brought to a successful conclusion, the acquisition should be integrated with determination, and as fast as possible according to a predetermined plan, using as the spearhead a project team with membership from both companies. The aim must be to maximize the value of the enlarged enterprise, through the early realization of the anticipated synergies, whilst at the same time minimizing the inevitable impact of culture shock on the acquired company. Since culture shock of some kind is inevitable, it should be anticipated and mechanisms put in place to stimulate and motivate the key members of the acquired company, thereby giving them the personal incentive to deal effectively with their own culture shock in a positive manner.

If the above steps are carried out thoroughly and carefully, the inevitable risks attendant on any acquisition should be reduced to a minimum.

In general the acquisition strategy is one that should be employed with great caution. The more closely related the business of the acquisition candidate is to the business of the acquiror, typically the less the risk there is, since the new owner will be familiar with the major problems likely to be encountered, and experienced in dealing with them. An acquisition of an unfamiliar company in an unrelated area of business from both a market and a product viewpoint is therefore the highest-risk strategy of all, and should be resisted if at all possible.

The major exception to this general rule is when the acquiring company's core competence is in company appraisal, acquisition and financial management (e.g. Hanson). In this case such a company can legitimately claim to be operating in the area it knows best, that is, the bottom left quadrant of the options cube (Figure 7.4), even if the products and markets of the company to be acquired are not familiar.

7.8 Summary

Both alliances and acquisition strategies are generally pursued by companies in order to strengthen their chances of achieving sustainable competitive advantage by providing them with a stronger Producer Matrix position in terms of both effectiveness and efficiency. They hope thereby to strengthen their position on the Customer Matrix, which is the ultimate arbiter of competitive success. The strategies are not necessarily mutually exclusive, and in fact the lowest-risk approach is probably to form an alliance in order to get to know a partner better, possibly before acquiring it. An alliance for its own sake, and not followed by acquisition, is also, however, an appropriate competitive strategy if it strengthens Producer and Customer Matrix positioning.

8

Implementation through internal development

We now revert to the lowest risk of the 'how?' options: internal development. This option is particularly appropriate if the company is financially strong, well endowed with competences, and time is not critical in putting a new product on the market. Internal development has the advantages of control and familiarity. With good timing and judgement, it can confer first-mover advantages, and it preserves the know-how within the firm. However, it is also limiting: it prevents access being obtained to external competences, resources and the stimuli of new ideas. In all but the largest companies it also limits development for reasons of financial constraints, and in all cases it makes the path a long one from the development of the idea to having the product on the market. Development solely through internal activity can therefore be slow, and one mistake with a major new product may well be disproportionately damaging to the firm's future.

The most critical issue in managing strategic change is the level of team commitment to effecting the required changes. Without a high level of commitment, the changes are unlikely to be implemented. We have argued (Chapter 1) that one way to generate commitment is through the involvement of managers in the strategy-making process. If they feel genuinely involved in its development, they are likely to be committed to the resulting strategy. However, involvement may not be enough to trigger change. A useful way of exploring the likelihood of real change taking place is the model set out in Figure 8.1. The four elements of the model are as follows:

A. Dissatisfaction with the existing situation.

Figure 8.1 A model of strategic change

B. A clear and understandable future strategy.

C. Identifiable first steps towards the future strategy.

D. The costs of changing, both in a monetary and psychological sense, for instance fear, insecurity at doing new things differently and so forth.

The model is multiplicative, which means that if any of the elements A, B or C is zero, no change occurs. For example, if the top team comes up with a good and clear competitive strategy (B) and a set of actions that would move the organization towards the vision (C), but they are not sufficiently dissatisfied with the status quo, then no change will take place. It is for this reason that executives brought in to achieve a turnaround often go out of their way to simulate a crisis, for only in a crisis situation will they receive a mandate from all the stakeholders to make uncomfortable changes. Similarly, if there is dissatisfaction (A) and a clear strategy (B) but no-one can see what the next steps should be to help move towards the strategy (C), then again nothing happens.

This simple but powerful model helps us to understand why strategic change might not be happening, despite general agreement to it. It also indicates where the efforts need to be focused in order to bring about strategic change, that is, to reduce complacency (A), clarify what needs to be done (B, C) or to tackle the problems of the real or imagined costs of change (D).

8.1   Implementation

The existing structures and processes in the organization support the current ways of doing things. If the strategy indicates that the organization needs to behave in different ways, there are likely to be problems should the existing structures be used to implement the changes. Current structures and processes may well distort and dilute the intended strategy to the point where no discernible change takes place.

Many firms are organized on a functional basis; that is, there are separate departments for manufacturing, engineering, sales, procurement, etc. If the strategy is implemented through the existing functional structure, the intended strategy will be interpreted by functional managers in terms that make sense to them, and in ways that reflect the type of activities the function has previously been responsible for. However, it may be that critical actions are required which fall outside the traditional functional division of labour. If the strategy is only translated into behaviour that reflects the past functional specialization, then actions that lie outside the existing functions (or, more typically, actions that cut across several existing functions) are not going to be identified and carried out.

It may therefore be necessary to employ other structures and processes if significant changes to routine behaviour are required. If structures and processes that lie outside the status quo are used, this should reduce the possibility that the intended strategy will become assimilated into the existing routines, and thus reduced in its impact.

The functional structure is appropriate for performing the basic tasks of the firm, but as this organizational form is probably common to all firms in a given industry, it cannot deliver extraordinary task performance to achieve lowest costs and highest PUV. Processes other than the conventional structural specialization must be involved in delivering competitive advantage.

There are a number of ways in which organizations use processes outside the existing structures to effect change. Four popular approaches are the following:

- Competence champions.
- Project management.
- Cross-functional teams.
- Reorganizing the structure.

Competence champions

Here the actions that are required to move the organization towards the intended strategy are grouped into broad competences. Examples of these required competences might be the following:

- To achieve lowest delivered cost.
- To attract and retain well-motivated, well-qualified staff.

- To achieve rapid new product introductions.
- To maximize the profitable business opportunities available in the after-market.

It is the role of the competence champion to drive the agreed sets of actions required to develop each competence. He/she should be held accountable by the chief executive officer (CEO) and the top team for progress towards the achievement of this competence. The actions usually involve staff from several different functions working together in small teams, which means that, in order to have influence over staff from other departments, the champion must have the appropriate authority. This can be achieved in two ways:

- Either the competence champions are selected from the group of top managers. Thus they would carry the formal authority of their functional positions.
- Or the competence champions are selected from a pool of high-flying middle/senior managers (so they have their own skills and abilities to influence people who may be senior to them), but they are visibly empowered by the CEO. They should have a direct reporting line to the CEO.

Project management

Project management is a well-established discipline that has evolved as a result of the problems of managing large-scale, one-off projects (e.g. building a dam, sending a man to the moon). It requires clear separation of the client role from that of project manager. The client sets the objective for the project, and is the ultimate judge of its success. The client can terminate the project at any time. The project manager is usually assigned a multi-disciplinary project team to carry out the project. The composition of the team may change as the project moves through its stages. The project must have a tangible and measurable outcome, that is, an end to work towards. The project needs to be broken down into a sequence of tasks, which can be scheduled and controlled.

The role of project manager differs from that of 'competence champion' as the project manager is responsible for a clearly defined set of actions that have a definite end point. The development of competences is more likely to be an open-ended ongoing responsibility; however, it is likely that discrete projects may be set up to help in the development of competences.

The advantages of the project management technique in strategy implementation derive from the disciplines and procedures that have been developed: the fact that it is a multi-disciplinary approach and the measurability of the outputs. Not all the changes that are required to implement a strategy successfully can be managed in this way, but if the basic disciplines of project management can be introduced into the organization, then the more tasks that can be managed through these processes, the greater the likelihood that significant strategic change can be effected.

Cross-functional teams

Every organizational structure is a compromise. If you specialize by function you reap the advantages of expertise, at the cost of a client, product or market focus. If you specialize by product market you may fall below the necessary critical mass for skill specialization. Cross-functional teams can be used to overcome some of the disadvantages of functional structures. However, if they are to work they must be managed in a special way:

- They need clear, broad, stable but challenging goals or 'missions'.
- They need to be left alone to get on with the job.
- They must have 'heavyweight' leaders who have influence.
- It is important that the members of the team are able to 'deliver' the function they represent: that is, they must be powerful enough to make decisions that commit their function.
- Team contributions must be recognized and rewarded by functional bosses.
- The work of teams may need to be coordinated.
- The team must be stable, to allow the members to establish good working relationships, and to develop a team spirit.

Reorganization

If any of the three processes described above are used, there may well come a point where the old functional groupings and specializations are found to be increasingly inappropriate for the changed direction of the organization. At some point the logic of the old structure becomes untenable, as more and more activity is driven by

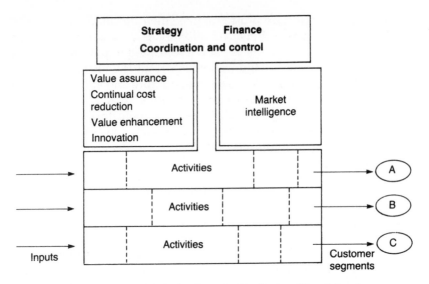

Figure 8.2 A structure for Sustainable Competitive Advantage

projects, and by cross-functional teams in pursuit of the required competences. The opportunity may present itself to acknowledge the fundamental shift in the focus of the organization by restructuring to bring the formal structure more in line with the actual work of the organization.

This may happen in small ways with the development of new specialisms like quality assurance, innovation, technology development and project and programme management. It may be advantageous to anticipate the evolution of new bases of specialization by deliberately reshaping the organization, if it is clear that in order to gain sustainable advantage the firm must develop outstanding competences in the following:

- New product introduction.
- Lowest delivered costs.
- Right-first-time quality.

It might be advantageous to recognize this formally by establishing groups that have as their primary responsibility the achievement of these three competences. This type of bold initiative can be extremely powerful in signalling a major shift in strategic direction.

Figure 8.2 depicts a generic structure for a firm aiming to achieve competitive advantage. The operating core of the organization consists of sets of linked activities which deliver Perceived Use Value to customers. In this example there are three main customer segments being served. The core activities might include, for example, sales, procurement, assembly, delivery and service, with strong coordination across these linked activities to ensure that customer needs are met.

The activity managers are responsible for delivering value to the customer at lowest cost. Because these priorities may be in conflict, these managers are supported by staff teams concerned with cost reduction (the 'continual cost reduction' team) and with value assurance (note that the terminology used describes as accurately as possible the role of the group). Value enhancement refers to staff who are concerned with continually improving the Perceived Use Value of the firm's products or services. By using information supplied by the 'market intelligence' group, this team can help direct the development of new products and services driven by accurate information about changing customer needs and competitor positioning.

The apex of the organization has three basic functions to perform: the first and most critical is strategy development, for example searching for new market or product opportunities; the second is the management of the finances of the business; the third is strategic control and coordination across the whole business.

This type of structure looks quite different from older, more functional forms of organization. The major advantage of this form is that it is derived from the demands of competitive strategy. Note that there are no functions like 'management accounts', 'personnel', 'administration' or 'public relations'. Unless the activity can be seen to be either adding Perceived Use Value or helping to reduce costs, it should be eliminated. No doubt some activities of the management accounts department would still be required (the gathering and analysis of cost information, for example) but this activity takes place within the cost reduction team, the nomenclature being deliberately selected to focus attention on the team's contribution.

8.2 Identifying blockages to change

A 'force-field' approach can be useful in trying to implement competitive strategy (see Figure 8.3). The future organization is represented by the broken wavy line, the current situation is the solid wavy line. There are forces acting in the organization that are

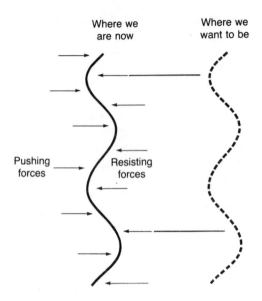

Figure 8.3   Force-field analysis

already moving the firm in the right direction (e.g. we are already engaged in extensive training in quality assurance, shop floor attitudes seem to be in favour of some changes). However, set against these pushing forces are resisting forces, or blockages to change. To bring these to the surface the management team will have to engage in some challenging thinking, and they will need to be very open, honest and explicit. If a major blockage is the cynical attitude of the finance director towards any new initiatives, then this must be raised and confronted. If the autocratic CEO is seen to be stifling initiatives, then this must be brought out into the open and discussed. Not all blockages will be of this sensitive nature, but they may nevertheless be difficult to identify. As we argued earlier, routines dominate organizational behaviour. Ways must be found to surface and to critique routine ways of doing things.

Some suggestions here might be to take a typical activity and to conduct a type of value-engineering exercise on it. We should ask the following questions:

- Why is this done at all? Does it contribute to either reducing costs or delivering value? If the answer is not clear, then maybe it need not be done at all.

- Should we be doing this ourselves? Could it be subcontracted?

- Why is this done this way?
- Who else could or should be involved in this activity?
- How else could the activity be performed?
- What other activities does this one affect directly?

Questions like these may help to surface some of the taken-for-granted routines which may be impediments to change.

The culture web explained in Chapter 4 can be helpful in trying to identify blockages to change. A culture web for the current organization can be constructed by, for example, getting several small teams of managers to brainstorm their views about the elements of the organization's culture; the power structures, both formal and informal, the organization structure, control and reward systems, key routines and ritualistic behaviour, stories and myths, symbols and role models. The paradigm is usually more difficult to surface, being the beliefs and assumptions, held in common, but taken for granted in the firm. These beliefs may be so ingrained in the firm that they are rarely discussed, yet they may refer to such changing elements as customer needs or competitor strengths. For example it may be surmised that managers at Rolls-Royce in Crewe would believe that customers place great store on the fact that all parts are made in Crewe and not bought in. Yet if a survey were to show that customers were far more concerned with the image and quality of the car than with the origin of the parts, this would potentially pave the way for a radical reconfiguration of Rolls-Royce's activity cost or value chain, and enable a far lower cost configuration to be adopted.

By comparing the cultural webs produced by the teams, it is usually possible to discern common features, suggesting some common perceptions of the firm's culture. The web can then be used to identify blockages to change.

One way of doing this is to develop a view of the type of organization that would, ideally, be set up to compete most effectively in the chosen markets, that is, to answer the question: What is the required organization to deliver the competitive strategy? What skills and competences would it have? What structures, processes, systems and information would it need? What culture, values and management styles would be appropriate? The vision of the required organization can then be compared with the existing one. This process frequently highlights the major blockages to change that would have to be removed in order to achieve the required organization. A simple chart like Figure 8.4 can be used to summarize this analysis. The 'extent of change' can be assessed on a

	Required organization	Actual organization	Extent of change	Possible actions
Skills and resources				
Structure, systems and information				
Culture, style and values				

1 = Minor change
5 = Major change

Figure 8.4 Assessing the extent of required change

1–5 scale, where 5 is a major change and 1 a minor one. Ideas about possible action can be jotted down in the last column.

Once the major pushing and resisting forces have been identified, they can be rated according to their perceived strength or importance. This can be represented in Figure 8.3 by the length of the arrow.

The pace of movement towards the required organization can be increased by one of the following strategies:

- Strengthening the pushing force (e.g. extending the quality programme to include all staff).
- Adding new pushing forces (setting up a new product development task force to explore ways of reducing the time to market).
- Reducing the resisting forces (fire the finance director).

In this way tangible actions can be identified, again by getting managers to think creatively, which cumulatively will accelerate progress towards the achievement of the strategy.

8.3   Prioritizing and ownership

Managers are busy people: even if they are supposed to be spending their days managing the strategy of the organization, the chances are that they will be bogged down in day-to-day operational activity.

The management group have, therefore, a limited capacity to do new things and to drive new initiatives. This scarce management resource must, therefore, be deployed to best advantage.

The actions derived from the processes described above must be prioritized. This can be done in a systematic way, by identifying which actions impinge on the achievement of more than one competence, and then by rating how well this is currently performed. Alternatively, the managers can agree on a subset of actions to be tackled first. This selection should be guided by the following principles:

- Select actions that can be accomplished fairly easily. (An early success is vital.) If there is demonstrable success in tackling an action, this can encourage others to try new ways of doing things, and the momentum of change can be built up.

- Select an action that has powerful symbolic qualities. Do something that clearly signals to people that things are changing, and that the organization is breaking away from the past.

Each prioritized action must be owned by an individual, preferably a volunteer, not a 'pressed man'. Collective ownership rarely works. Some person must feel himself/herself accountable for delivering the action. This is necessary in order to encourage a busy manager to find the space to work on the things that need changing. Without this accountability, the day-to-day demands of the job will drive out the good intentions of the managers. A manager must be accountable, but this does not necessarily mean he/she is responsible for effecting the actions: the owner of the action may need to convene a small team from within his/her department or from across the organization to implement the required actions.

There must be an agreed timetable of deadlines for the achievement of each action, and managers must be held to account for progress towards the required results. The strategy implementation process should be periodically reviewed, and the timetable revised to take note of the most recent developments. This review should seek to confirm the broad strategic direction set out in the mission statement, and managers should share their experience of trying to implement the required changes. They may identify some common blockages, to change which may require new actions to be mounted. Sharing experiences of implementation successes can help others get ideas, and should boost morale.

Lastly, the control and reward systems should reflect the intentions of the strategy statement. There is little point in having a strategy statement that says that 'We aim to delight our customers' if there is no genuine attempt to measure the firm's performance against this objective. If the control systems still emphasize other variables, such as percentage of budget used, capacity utilization, overhead recovery and gross margin, then staff will direct their efforts towards these measures, not to achieving 'delighted customers'. To take another example, if the strategy statement states that 'We aim to have an organization that our staff can be proud of', then this must be operationalized in some way. First, it is necessary to know what would make the staff proud to work in the firm, then to set about changing things so that they become proud of their organization. Ways must be found, perhaps through staff surveys, to measure how well this important aim is being achieved.

Similarly, rewards must be in tune with the intentions set out in the mission. Staff must be recognized and rewarded for behaviour that is clearly in line with the mission: if an employee stays on late to solve a customer's problem, this must be recognized. If a group, using their initiative, comes up with a way of achieving major savings in material costs, it should be appropriately rewarded. If it is important to shift the organization away from a conservative, 'toe the line, keep your nose clean' culture, to one where people are free to experiment, take risks and assume responsibility, it is vital that individuals who display these qualities are encouraged and promoted.

8.4   Building versus demolishing

We have deliberately concentrated our attention in this chapter on the most difficult aspects of managing strategic change. These are the changes that require the organization to behave in different ways, to learn new things and to develop new attitudes. But there is another category of strategic changes which is essentially about eliminating or reducing aspects of the business; for example, closing an inefficient plant, sacking a layer of management, halving the range of products, withdrawing from unprofitable client relationships, eliminating a shift or closing the research department.

These changes may well be painful for the individuals directly affected, but they are of a quite different nature from those changes which are concerned with building new competences. There is no doubt that dramatic changes such as those mentioned above can be effected rapidly, and that such changes can have a powerful influence on the attitudes and behaviour of those that remain in the organization; but in comparison to the problems of building competences, even quite draconian changes are fairly straightforward to implement.

8.5 Summary

Strategic change through internal development involves the least risk for the firm, but suffers from the disadvantages of frequently taking a lengthy period to see results, and generally suffering from the limitations of resource constraints.

Where internal change of a major nature is attempted it can rarely be achieved entirely through the conventional organization structure, since this has been developed to carry out the existing strategy. Such devices as competence champions, project management, cross-functional teams and internal restructuring may be useful in attempting to change the way in which the firm behaves. Changing behavioural routines represents a far larger challenge than even major one-off changes like closing a factory or selling a subsidiary. The latter is akin to surgery and the necessary actions are easy to see; the former is closer to attempting to keep New Year resolutions. It is all too easy to fall back into the old way of doing things. The above organizational devices are intended to prevent such recidivism.

9

Conclusion

In this short book we have attempted to explore the **essence** of competitive strategy. In trying to distil this essence from the huge volume of work that has been done in this field, we have had to make difficult decisions about what to put in and what to leave out. We have also come to the view that existing frameworks and methods do not adequately address some of the key issues in competitive strategy, and so we have attempted to develop some new techniques, in particular the Customer and Producer Matrices.

These two devices reflect the basic economic relationships between demand (customers' PUV) and supply (producer competences). The two matrices represent the two different perspectives on competitive strategy that predominate in the literature; the market-based approach (the Customer Matrix) and the resource-based theory (the Producer Matrix). It is our firmly held view that both perspectives are necessary, and are indeed inseparable, if one is to gain a thorough understanding of competitive strategy, in the sense of the unending quest for sustainable competitive advantage for a product or service in a market. To advocate only one approach is similar to taking a view that one blade of a pair of scissors is more important than the other. Clearly both blades are required, if the cloth is to be cut at all.

The Customer and Producer Matrices form the core of our contribution. We have shown how these concepts can be operationalized, and how, given the right kind of information, they can be used to determine the main thrusts of a firm's strategy, and to enable the strategist to gain insights into market needs, the firm's competences and the relative strengths of the competition.

In order to develop a longer-term perspective, tools like five-force analysis, PEST and scenario building can be useful, particularly in broadening the competitive strategy debate. A range of competitive strategy options is described in Chapter 6, and a straightforward method for evaluating them in specific situations is described.

Chapters 7 and 8 address the 'How?' question that the strategist must face before turning the strategy into action. He must consider the three basic alternative ways of implementing strategy: through joint development, acquisition or internal development, or perhaps some combination of all three. In all the options under consideration, the importance of assessing the relative risks of different courses of action is stressed.

Although these topics have been dealt with in a logical sequence in the book, in practice the evolution of a competitive strategy is likely to be a more complex process, involving several iterations between analysis, formulation and evaluation. As more and better-quality information is accumulated, for instance on customer needs and on competitors, opinions will change, and in the process of determining strategy, care must be taken to build consensus and commitment within the management team.

We would suggest the following guidelines for a management team seeking to improve its firm's competitive strategy.

1. Take time out. Even very senior managers find their days dominated by short-term operational issues. When managers meet, the agenda often tends to be driven by short-term concerns. In these circumstances 'strategy' tends to be more of an emergent, reactive or opportunistic process, rather than something that results from an explicit attempt to debate and decide the firm's future direction. Hence the need to set time aside specifically to debate strategy, and ideally away from day-to-day concerns.

2. Involve the team. Commitment to strategic change is enhanced where individual managers feel they have had some involvement in deciding the strategic direction to be taken. So the key members of the management team should be genuinely involved in the strategy debate, and should usually initiate the ideas which are subsequently evaluated.

3. Be challenging. To be balanced against the advantages of team involvement in strategy determination is the frequent disadvantage of the adoption of narrow parochial attitudes. These need to be challenged, as do the taken-for-granted assumptions that are often such a limiting factor in the firm's culture. The process of developing insights that help to throw off cultural limitations can be helped by the following practices:

- Involving an outsider in the debate, a consultant, a non-executive director or perhaps a member of HQ staff.
- Assigning the role of devil's advocate to a member of the team. This person's role is to be critical and challenging to the assumptions underpinning the discussions. It is important to rotate this role, so that one team member is not perceived as being continually negative.
- Gathering accurate facts about the firm's competitive position and its competitors, as well as on customer preferences and perceptions and industry analysts' views. Hard data in these areas can help to keep the team close to reality; neither unduly optimistic nor depressingly pessimistic.

4. Expect the process to take time. The process of devising a competitive strategy cannot be done overnight, or in one workshop session. Normally time needs to be taken after a workshop to gather better-quality information, and then to build consensus and commitment; the crafting of the ultimate strategy is of course a never-ending task.

5. Summarize the essence of the strategy. The essential features of the strategy should be summarized in some form of 'strategy statement'. This internal document can then be used by other parts of the firm in helping them determine their roles in delivering the strategy. The statement should be precise, unambiguous, free of platitudes and 'motherhood' statements, and available to all firm members. It should rarely exceed one sheet of paper in length.

6. Agree priorities and ownership. It is essential that the actions required to start the implementation of the chosen strategy are prioritized, and that each action is 'owned' by a named individual. This is necessary to help ensure that managers find the time to work on the strategic actions and to avoid day-to-day imperatives driving out strategic action and purpose.

7. Continually keep the strategy under review. Strategy is not a once-a-year activity. The strategy should be continually kept under review, and progress in effecting the necessary changes should be measured and controlled. If the strategy has resulted from a robust and critical debate, it should stand up to regular challenge and, barring dramatic unforeseen events, the essential features of the strategy should remain stable over a period of time, at least two years.

It is worth stating that almost any strategy is preferable to no strategy at all. Some sense of direction is better than aimless drifting, driven by reactions to day-to-day events. A 'perfect' strategy is probably not attainable, as the future is not knowable, but the sense of direction that results from a critical analysis of the firm's competitive position, and the exercise of informed judgement is likely of itself to give the team a focused sense of purpose, and a feeling of empowerment.

References

Grant, R. M. (1991) 'The resource-based theory of competitive advantage: Implications for strategy formulation', *California Management Review* Spring, 114–35.

Johnson, G. and K. Scholes (1993) *Exploring Corporate Strategy*, 3rd edn, Hemel Hempstead: Prentice Hall.

Pfeffer, J. and G. Salancik (1978) *The External Control of Organizations*, New York: Harper.

Porter, M. E. (1980) *Competitive Strategy*, New York: The Free Press.

Porter, M. E. (1985) *Competitive Advantage*, New York: The Free Press.

Porter, M. E. (1987) 'From competitive advantage to corporate strategy', *Harvard Business Review* May/June, 43–59.

Rumelt, R. P. (1991) 'How much does industry matter?', *Strategic Management Journal* 12 March 1991, 167–85.

Index